Buddy Stall

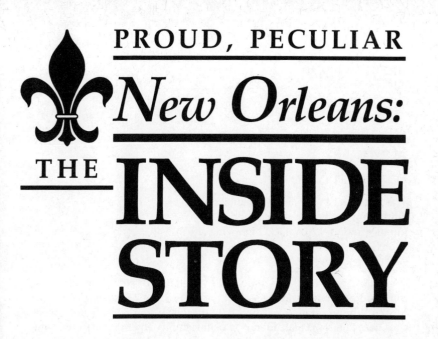

PROUD, PECULIAR

New Orleans:

THE INSIDE STORY

GASPAR J. "Buddy" STALL

Foreword by Pete Fountain

Claitor's Publishing Division
Baton Rouge, Louisiana

ACKNOWLEDGEMENTS:

Myron Tassin, Publishing Consultant
Shirley Tassin, Editorial Assistance
John Desmond, FAIA; Jacket Drawing (1970)

SPECIAL THANKS TO:

Don and Lynda Knecht, George and Darnell Braud, Pete Fountain, Stanton "Buddy" Frazar and the staff of the Historic New Orleans Collection; Murial Whitney, Laine Caistex, Bob and Olga Bourgeois, Mrs. Harriet Callahan, Louisiana State Library; Collin Hammer and the staff of the New Orleans Public Library; Calvin Balencie, Noel Blakley, Joe Cahn, the New Orleans School of Cooking; Joe Bush, New Orleans City Park; Beverly Gianna, New Orleans Tourist Commission; Henry Gondolfo, Metairie Cemetery; Jimmy Fitzmorris, Joe Gemelli; Nash Roberts, Channel 6; Al Hirt, Joseph C. Madere; Gayle Burchfield, Louisiana Office of Tourism; Bob LeBlanc.

To Maw Maw Margaret,
the mother of my children,
the grandmother of my children's children
and the "chord" that binds us all together.

Aerial view shows clearly why New Orleans is known as the Crescent City.

*T*able *of Contents*

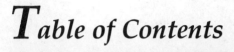

Pete Fountain

Foreword

by Pete Fountain

When Gaspar "Buddy" Stall approached me about writing the foreword for a book of vignettes about the little-known, hard to believe personality traits of New Orleans, my first inclination was to say, "Hasn't it been done?" However, given an opportunity to read a few chapters, I quickly realized that here was a real contribution to understanding why New Orleans is such a fun city, why it is so different, why its people are so proud and, yes, a little peculiar in the eyes of those who don't understand.

I have a friend who, like the leading character in the Pulitzer Prize winning book *A Confederacy of Dunces*, develops a visible case of nervous insecurity whenever he has to leave his beloved city. In fact, this geographic recluse prefers to stay in the "Old City," the Vieux Carré laid out by Bienville in the early 1700s. To him, it's the center of the universe. Here's a man who wouldn't care in the least if the world stopped at the edge of town. To an outsider, this man is peculiar; to Orleanians, he's typical of thousands of proud people who adorn this jewel on the Mississippi. They understand.

Buddy Stall is one who understands well. His lifelong dedication to collecting and disseminating the inside story of this alluring mistress on the river has become nothing short of a fixation . . . an obsession bordering on mania.

Until now Stall's efforts have been limited mostly to teaching and making speeches to local organizations, including the Pete Fountain Half Fast Walking Club, plus regional, national and international conventioneers who come to the Crescent City to savor its charms. After his speeches, however, members of his audiences invariably want more than the time allows. Hence this effort to put his most interesting brush strokes between two covers.

Before reading *The Inside Story*, I thought I knew New Orleans. I felt I was quite well informed on the intricate variations of her personality. After all, her blood, along with Jack Daniels and *Pouilly Fuisse*, has flowed through my veins for a lifetime.

A few hours with Buddy Stall's inside story made me realize how little I really knew about her. From naughty ladies to nifty ones; red beans and rice to muffuletta sandwiches; Creoles versus Americans; voodoo and torture; criminal and prostitute immigrants; jazz funerals and water-filled graves; nuns braving storms, pirates and alligators to serve in New Orleans; yellow fever and malaria cutting down thousands, 8,000 Irish workers dying like flies . . . the past came back so vividly.

In New Orleans generations of hardship are quickly left behind; you can see it in the smiles of the people, especially senior citizens, as you walk along the store fronts of Canal Street. Their faces mirror a *joie de vivre* unmistakenly New Orleans.

As the people laugh they do it heartily, as if their body language is proclaiming with joy, delight and optimism: "Hey, I'm happy; I live in New Orleans." Buddy Stall reminds us of why we're so inclined to smile and laugh and love.

CHAPTER ONE

*F*ood;
Guide to
Excellent Restaurants

Since the head table is always served first, an after-dinner speaker is usually finished with dessert before some in the audience have even begun the entrée. Thus, a lot of time is spent talking to the people around you.

After 25 years of such dialogue with visitors from out-of-town, out-of-state and out-of-country, I have had ample opportunity to filter out the four major misconceptions outsiders have of the New Orleans area:

1. First-time visitors are surprised to find that our city is not located on the Gulf of Mexico.
2. They are amazed that none of our natives have a true deep-south drawl, and that many have a definite Brooklyn accent.
3. The majority think all Creoles are black people, and this, of course, is completely erroneous.
4. Since our city was founded by the French, newcomers expect Crescent City cuisine to be strictly French, and are confounded when they find that it most definitely is not.

New Orleans is the only city in the United States with a cuisine peculiarly and distinctly its own; it is not French, Spanish, Haitian, Latin American, German, Irish, Italian, African, West Indian or any other nationality per se. It is delectable New Orleans cooking that can be found nowhere else.

There are many reasons why our cuisine is unique. As a port city, New Orleans was a (if not *the*) leading melting pot in North America. With its location east of the Rocky Mountains, hordes of immigrants wishing to migrate West, or East for that matter, used the Port of New Orleans as a jumping-off point.

Many who came liked the city too much to leave. That pattern still holds today. A great many who came to our city in the 1960s to work in the NASA rocket plant chose to remain in New Orleans upon completion of their assignments.

Records indicate that before the Civil War 68 different nationalities lived in New Orleans. Each of these had its own traditional foods and ways of preparing them and, of course, was proud of its culinary heritage. Italians living next to Germans, wishing to share their favorite recipes, swapped with their neighbors; before long a completely new taste was melded. Add those two nationalities to 66 others and you begin to appreciate how New Orleans' food evolved into a very distinctive flavor. Gumbo is a prime example.

Gumbo is considered truly New Orleans and is a favorite of local people as well as the many visitors who have partaken of this delicious concoction. It was made possible by Africans who came to New Orleans on slave ships. One of their favorite native foods was called *kingombo* (okra). Some hid the seed of the kingombo plant in their African hairdos and smuggled them to their new homes around New Orleans. They planted the seeds, tended the plants and prepared the yield for appreciative masters who liked it so much they introduced the course to their friends. Since the African gumbo did not have seafood in it, one wishing to use local epicurean delights—available in large quantities from the surrounding marshes and Gulf—added oysters, shrimp, crabs, and voilà: seafood gumbo!

The Choctaw Indians gave it their own flavor, which became the best-known of all gumbos because of a popular song which introduced the word *filé* (pronounced fee-lay) to the nation. Filé is an Indian herb, a powder made by pulverizing dried sassafras leaves. The filé powder is added to the gumbo after it is cooked to give a distinctive flavor and body. It is also used as a thickener for soups and stews. Filé is still a popular herb used by many of the area's Creole cooks.

The three best-known varieties of gumbo, although there are many others, are: the okra gumbo, given to us by the African slaves; filé gumbo, which was concocted by the Choctaw Indians; and of course, seafood gumbo, believed to be made popular by the Cajuns who were the leading area fishermen.

There is no doubt that the French, the founders of New Orleans, played a most important role in the city's daily eating habits. From the very beginning the Creoles considered cooking the highest of the home arts. They called it "gullet science" and their favorite expression was: "An empty sack cannot stand alone."

Considering that a sixteen-year-old has spent three years of life eating, it should be an enjoyable experience. I, for one, am grateful that the French founders along with the Spaniards who later ruled our city, were such fanatics about the quality of the food they consumed. One historian observed that Spanish cuisine was elevated almost to the same level of importance as conquest.

The French brought the Ursuline nuns to educate their young girls—which in the 1700s meant cooking, the wifely arts and then if time permitted, reading, writing and arithmetic. Then, French Canadian Madame Langlois, the mother of Creole cooking, learned much from the Indians and passed this information on to the ladies of New Orleans. Spanish leaders, many of them coming from their colonies in Mexico and Latin America, brought with them their own beloved Iberian dishes. These they supplemented with the culinary secrets they had acquired from the conquered Incas and the Aztecs and with the condiments they learned to enjoy from the Caribbean. As each nationality came to our city it made its own contribution to New Orleans gastronomical art.

The single most influential factor leading to New Orleans' rise to international prominence in the culinary arts came about because of the French Revolution. In 1793 Louis XVI and his lovely queen both lost their heads to the guillotine. Before the revolution was over many noble families suffered the same fate. Every wealthy family had its own private chef with his small army of assistants and his treasured file of ingenious dishes for which he was famous. These private chefs, with so many aristocratic appetites lost to the guillotine, were forced to other less-proud pursuits. Some

Crawfish bisque is a thick soup laced generously with crawfish heads stuffed with a dressing of chopped, seasoned crawfish tails. (Louisiana Tourist Commission)

migrated to the little Paris of America, New Orleans, and either cooked for the wealthy or opened restaurants. Here they found the same level of appreciation for their art as they had enjoyed in their homeland. To New Orleans these great chefs brought their secret recipes, the finesse of French sauces and subtlety of seasonings. They were captivated by the fact that the people of New Orleans lived to eat and did not simply eat to live.

By 1793 the city was on its way to having some of the best gourmet food on the planet. And it has improved steadily each year until today. A plain boiled potato, vegetable or shrimp is as out of place in New Orleans as snow skis, ice skates and a sled.

The era following the 1793 migration of the great chefs of France to New Orleans was followed by what is called the Golden Age of the South. Those 50 years between the admission of Louisiana to the Union and the Civil War were glorious times for some— especially for the gourmet. This was the era of affluent cotton and sugar planters and the attendant grand manner during which Louisiana boasted of having more millionaires than all the other states in the nation combined.

During this period plantations around New Orleans were trying to outdo each other in elegance and in the number of parties that were held. Some operated on the scale of hotels and created dishes for the most discriminating class of epicures in the history of America.

To Creole cooking, Negro cooks added mysterious touches from Africa and the West Indies and blended the flavors of accumulated contributions of the previous century into hundreds of mouth-watering recipes that pleased the palate and later crowded Creole cookbooks.

Because of the tremendous wealth of the city before the Civil War the custom of dining out regularly became extremely popular in New Orleans around 1830. It was not in good social taste to eat at home too often. People would eat out simply to show they were affluent. Dining out provided an opportunity to be seen, and the fine restaurants that were springing up all over the city were bulging with the upper crust.

In 1840 a young man named Antoine Alciatore, of Marseilles, France—a finished chef before heading for New Orleans— came to the city and opened his world-famous restaurant, Antoine's. The timing on Antoine's part was most opportune because of the phenominal wealth of the city. Elaborate suppers and after-theatre dinners were the rage of the day and Antoine's capitalized on it to the fullest. In 1899 Jules Alciatore, his son, created a new oyster dish that became world renowned. He called it Oysters Rockefeller because it was as rich in flavor as the Rockefellers were in finance. Every great chef will tell you that to create a new dish is more important to the happiness of mankind than to find a new star. Jules wanted to be long remembered. And Antoine's continues to remind us of him 85 years after his stroke of genius.

Because of their vast contributions to the pleasures of the people of New Orleans, the chefs who ply their profession here are regarded with the same esteem as are the superstars of sports and show business.

NEW ORLEANS FOOD FOR ALMOST ALL OCCASIONS
As a Wedding Gift

Cooking was so high on the Creole's list that the greatest gift a young girl could receive from her mother was a set of iron pots she had used for several years. Their prior use assured that they were well-seasoned.

Food and Religion

The Creoles mixed religion with food and folklore. For example, it was believed that if you visited seven different churches on Good Friday and ate gumbo herbs made from seven different greens, fortune would smile on you for the balance of the year.

Food and Sports

Food was used as part of the sporting ritual in the days when dueling was allowed. Since most duels were held early in the morning, before any Creole gentleman went on the field of honor he would first have black coffee and bread to fortify himself for what was to come, as well as against the dampness. The bread he ate was a small, hard-crusted loaf with a cylinder-like shape, about four to five inches long and two to three inches in diameter. Since the pistol was one of the instruments used most often in duels and the little short French roll looked something like a small pistol, the mini-bread became known as a *pistolette*. Even though we no longer have dueling, we still have the pistolette.

Food and Mardi Gras—King Cake

Food has been used for hundreds of years in France and New Orleans to help celebrate Mardi Gras. One of these foods is called the King Cake. The shape has always been in the form of a huge ring, size depending upon the number of people who were to attend the balls that were held weekly from January 6 (Little Christmas) until Mardi Gras. At the stroke of midnight all the guests who were invited would be seated around an expensive dining table and each was served a piece of cake with a glass of champagne. Hidden cleverly within the cake was a bean or a pecan (today a plastic baby doll). If the finder was a lady she chose her king by presenting him with a bunch of violets. If the lucky one was a gentleman he would choose his queen by offering her the flower from his lapel. Once the king and queen were introduced the king then escorted his queen around the parlor for all to admire.

They would be king and queen until the following week, when the next ball was held. It was tradition that the king bear the entire expense of the ball for which he was king and to provide the next king cake. Also, tradition dictated that he present the queen with a gift of jewelry. This favor was the only one a Creole mother would allow her daughter to accept from any gentleman outside of marriage.

In many Creole homes it was not uncommon to see a small jewelry box containing either a half or a whole bean. In some instances the king requested half the bean, thereby leaving the queen with only one half to display as evidence of her reign.

Many of the traditions started by the Creoles are still part of the Mardi Gras tradition. The Twelfth Night Revelers are a Mardi Gras krewe which take their name from the twelfth night after Christmas, or January 6, the night the three kings visited the Christ child. The Revelers have been in existence since 1870 and have always chosen their royalty by the traditional method—the king cake. In the early years a real cake was used. Today a simulated cake with little wooden drawers (one contains a golden bean) is employed. The maids pull drawers to see who will get the golden bean and be queen of the ball.

The King Cake tradition is still alive and well. To satisfy the demand, McKenzie's Bakery and Randazzo's Bakery together make 5,000 king cakes per day during the carnival season. And keep in mind that New Orleans has over 100 bakeries, and they all make king cakes. It would be safe to estimate that over one million of them are consumed each carnival season in New Orleans.

Food for Medicinal Purposes

The Creoles used crushed crab and crawfish eyes to treat rashes. Banana leaves were applied to foreheads for headaches, and plantain leaves were used on open sores. Oak leaf tea was taken to fight diarrhea, and as horrible as it might sound, the Creoles also drank roach tea to cure lockjaw. Surely anyone with lockjaw, upon learning that he would have to swallow roach tea, either continued to have lockjaw . . . or recovered quickly before having to take the "cure."

Food Used to Pacify a Baby

It was a crude custom, most unusual for sure, but very effective; the Creoles would tie one end of a string around a piece of pork and the other end to the baby's foot. If the baby happened to choke on the piece of pork his kicking movements would jerk on the string and pull out the "pacifier."

Food Brought to Your Door

Before the days of supermarkets, and that was not many years ago, a person could sit on the front steps and buy virtually everything needed to feed the family.

While we hear the ding-dong lady from Avon today, our fathers and mothers heard the slogans, or as they were better known, "cries" from an oyster vendor carrying his merchandise in a tin pail:

Oyster man, oyster man,
Get your fresh oysters from the oyster man
Bring out your pitcher, bring out your can
Get your nice oysters from the oyster man.

Unfortunately, few vendors survive, but one still roaming the streets of New Orleans is the taffy man. He travels in a colorful wagon pulled by a faithful horse who no doubt knows the city better than most of its citizens. To get your attention the taffy man rings a loud bell that is easily recognizable. Like the one Pavlov used on his dog, the bell at once whets your appetite for the chocolate, strawberry and vanilla renditions.

During the holiday seasons of Thanksgiving and Christmas it was not unusual to see vendors driving live turkeys, chickens and geese through the streets for customers to make a selection. Unwrapped bread and milk were delivered to the door daily. The lady of the house would have to dust off the bread before serving it. Blackberries, strawberries, figs, vegetables, watermelons, ice cream, snowballs, fish, water, wine—if one sat on the front steps long enough, almost everything in the line of food would eventually parade by.

Many of the street vendors were very successful peddlers who made enough money to finance the opening of their own corner groceries. At one time, before the great supermarket expansion following World War II, New Orleans had over 4,000 neighborhood grocery stores. Most, for convenience, were on street corners. Almost all had a black book in which to record credit. They all gave lagniappe.* New Orleans still has, because of its strong neighborhood ties, more neighborhood or corner groceries per capita than any other city in the United States. But just as the steam locomotive was the beginning of the end of the steamboat, corner grocery stores were the beginning of the end for most street vendors.

The supermarket is already decimating the ranks of the corner grocery store. It's called progress, good or bad, but how many of us would choose to go back to "the good ole days"? In just a matter of time, we will have only giant supermarkets and quick convenience stores of the 7-Eleven variety. Sad but true!

---

*Lagniappe—something extra, like the thirteenth doughnut in a baker's dozen.

BREAD

Bread is one of those food items that visitors marvel over. And New Orleans' people, while taking it for granted, consume it in enormous quantities.

It is interesting to note that New Orleans consumes more French bread than any other city in the world, including Paris, France. It is ironic that although there were over 400 bakeries in New Orleans as little as 50 years ago, almost all of the French bread baked in New Orleans today is baked by only four concerns; two German and two Italian bakeries. Curiously, there are no longer any Frenchmen baking French bread in this fair city by the river.

An amusing story was told to me by a man who many old timers claim was the "greatest of the great" when it came to baking French bread. He was the late Leopold J. Sandbrink. The good German was owner of Sandbrink Bakery, located at 940 Desire Street and founded in 1883. As a young man working for his father, Gerhard, one of Leopold's jobs was to supervise the personnel responsible for treating the water to make the bread the following day. This was before the advent of water purification plants so all water consumed had to be treated by those who used it.

The black man whose job it was to "clarify" the water became ill and sent his son in his place. Advising Sandbrink that his father had given him all necessary instructions, he said he was ready to go to work. Going to the river, he filled the barrels, returned and treated the water "as instructed by his father." The next day the water was used and the bread was delivered to regular customers from house to house. Before finishing his deliveries Sandbrink was hailed by some very unhappy patrons who insisted he taste the bread. When he did his mouth drew up tightly and he immediately thought of the new man settling the water. Calmly he went back to the bakery and asked the replacement to show him how he had done the job. The black man said, "just as my poppa told me: one bucket of coal and one bucket of alum." Sandbrink was flabbergasted! The process called for one bucket of coal and one small scoop of alum (about 50 times less than a bucket). The young man begged for mercy, pleading that he not be fired, "or poppa will kill me." Sandbrink, still not excited, said he would not fire him, but to help him remember what happened when too

New Orleanians consume more french bread than any other city in the world. Ironically, the four bakeries producing most of the delicacy are German and Italian, not
French. (Noel Blakely)

much alum was used to settle the water, made him eat one whole loaf of the bread. As Mr. Sandbrink told me, "You know, he never made that mistake again" which may prove that there is a lot to be said for first-hand experience.

Other breads consumed in New Orleans are the poorboy, Italian bread, pistolette and square-sliced bread for sandwiches.

French bread is a wide, short, pointed, crispy bread which is truly close to being sinful when eaten. Poorboy bread is long and slender and was designed for specific use.

In the 1930s, during the great depression, large numbers of people had little money, even for food. Since times were so tough and money so short, Clovis and Denny Martin were inspired by the hard times to make a sandwich which would fill a man's belly for a nickel, and a bigger one which would keep him going for most of the day for a dime. Martin Brothers, the originators of the poorboy sandwich, originally used the pointed French bread for their new creation. They found, however, that the pointed ends resulted in waste. Besides, there was too much dough in the fluted, pointed end of the French bread. Clovis and his brother called on a good friend, master French-bread baker John Gendusa, to develop and bake a bread for the newly-invented poorboy sandwich. Gendusa filled their needs by baking a 30-inch loaf with less dough and with ends that were less pointed.

The poorboy sandwich was an instant success; Martin Brothers started out ordering 50 French bread loaves daily to produce 100 sandwiches. In a short time they were making and selling 9,000 poorboy sandwiches per day. A record day for Martin Brothers each year was always on Mardi Gras, and their biggest day ever recorded 21,000 sandwiches.

From the time Gendusa made the first special poorboy loaf and Martin Brothers started selling the famous poorboy sandwich, it took only six months to completely saturate the city and to make the poorboy the most talked-about and consumed sandwich in New Orleans. At its location on St. Claude and Touro streets, Martin Brothers was a spot with which all New Orleanians were familiar. Sadly, they are no longer in business, but the memory lingers on.

Everyone's tastes differ, but my favorite poorboy sandwich

is now and always has been from Parkway Bakery, located right alongside Bayou St. John. The building would never win an award, but eating a Parkway Bakery poorboy should be classified a mortal sin. It's so good it should be bad for you!

To some Orleanians a seven-course meal is a roast beef poorboy and a six-pack of Dixie beer. (Photo by Noel Blakely)

During the Martin Brothers poorboy era New Orleans had a large Italian population, and it was not long before that ethnic group's answer to the French poorboy was conceived.

There was a time in the city's history when, because of economic conditions, Italians almost filled the French Quarter. In fact, for a short time the French Quarter had a second name; it was called "Little Italy." Salvatore Tusa, owner of the Central Grocery on Decatur Street, began making a large sandwich that would compete with the poorboy; after all, there were as many Italians short of money as any other nationality. He made the sandwich with a round bread called muffuletta and named it the "muffuletta sandwich."

The eight-inch diameter bread topped with sesame seeds was cut in half and each side was coated with high-grade imported olive oil that not only had a marvelous flavor but also a distinctive aroma. To this were added generous layers of imported cheeses, ham and salami, then topped off with a homemade olive salad especially made by Central Grocery. In my estimation it has never been equaled.

One of these sandwiches with a bottle of Jumbo (a quart of a local soft drink), was sure to fill the stomach of the biggest eater, if not that of a small family.

The third indigenous New Orleans sandwich utilizes a square, light loaf which is not cut in half as customary. The loaf is eight inches long by approximately four inches wide. When baking is complete the top is sliced off and the inside dough is removed. Once the insides are removed the walls are covered with melted butter and the cavity is filled with crisp fried oysters, shrimp or fish. It is then sprinkled generously with ketchup and topped off with slices of dill pickle. This creation was originally called a "mediator." It earned its name as follows: A man who stayed out all night (usually on paydays), could buy one before going home and be certain of an amiable reception regardless of his transgressions. It was a handy peacemaker.

Today the custom continues, except we are no doubt better behaved and no longer in need of a mediator. The creation is today called the shrimp or oyster boat. My nomination for king of the shrimp/oyster boat is Lakeview Restaurant on Hayne Boulevard in New Orleans East.

NO MEAL IN NEW ORLEANS IS COMPLETE
WITHOUT COFFEE WITH CHICORY

The Creoles had a saying for almost everything. Regarding coffee, they said they liked it:

Black as the devil,
Strong as death,
Sweet as love,
And hot as hell!

Well that's the way it was usually served. Someone said coffee and chicory sometimes got so strong when slow dripped, a spoon of water at a time, that when finished the coffee would get up and get its own sugar.

Chicory, a cultivated leafy vegetable with a carrot-shaped root, has been a popular additive to New Orleans' coffee since the time of the Civil War. When the supply of coffee dwindled during the strife it was found that the root, when dried, roasted and ground, made an excellent addition to coffee. Thus, the supply of the then-expensive and scarce coffee bean could be doubled by combining the coffee with chicory. Our people became accustomed to this unique flavor and, even though coffee became available in large quantities after the war, continued to drink it with chicory.

Would you believe that New Orleans was 212 years old when it introduced the now-popular coffee break. On March 17, 1930, managers of the Delta steamship, then the Mississippi Shipping Company, summoned their 80 employees in the Hibernia Bank Building in downtown New Orleans and initiated a daily 3:30 p.m. coffee recess. Company scouts had found the custom to be very well received in Brazil and adopted the idea for its New Orleans office. No one is sure what this innovation did for efficiency, but it is noted that the gross national product is not rising very rapidly.

WINE WITH EACH COURSE, PLUS A SPECIAL ONE
MIDWAY TO SPUR THE APPETITE

Habits are, undeniably, extremely hard to break. For too many years New Orleans' drinking water supply was far from being what you would call fair or even palatable. Even as late as the twentieth century water was still being clarified by letting river water settle overnight in large drums after adding a bucket of coal and a scoop of alum. After overnight settling, one would use the clear water from the top and discard the sediment at the bottom.

Cleaning a cistern was no picnic either. When the water reservoir became dirty it became convenient to drink wine and other alcoholic beverages. So, drink we did and drink we do! Today the Mississippi River, our primary source of drinking water, is polluted to the point that we may not have to build any more bridges across it. Just a little more pollution and we can simply walk across.

To give a scenario of the quantities of wine served at a typical social dinner in the good old days, let us lay out each course and the wine that went with it.

To start off, one would be served raw oysters and a glass of *white wine*, followed by a bowl of soup and a glass of *sherry or Madeira*. Next on the menu was fish, with which was served a *heavy white wine*. At this, the halfway point, a special *Ponche Romaine* was poured to stimulate the appetite. Then was served a healthy portion of roast plus a large glass of *champagne*, followed by the game food of the day with a glass of *Burgundy*. Last of the dishes was dessert, which was always accompanied with a choice of one's favorite *liqueur*, followed by *café noir* (black coffee).

Oh, yes, an elegant evening was usually crowned with the serving of flamed *Petit Brûle*, a drink made from orange peel, *brandy*, sugar cubes and spices. The nostrils were filled with this magnificent aroma while the palate was refreshed with the delectable taste.

Of course, if after drinking the Petit Brûle a guest desired an additional drink his wish was expedited.

Today, partially because of the Carnival Season and Mardi Gras, New Orleanians consume per capita more champagne than any city on the earth. Pat O'Brien's, located in the French Quarter, is a favorite watering hole not only for Orleanians but for visitors from the world over. New Orleans receives an estimated seven million visitors per year, and Pat O'Brien's gets its fair share of that number. The unequaled popularity of the establishment has earned for it the distinction of dispensing more liquid libation than any other bar in the world. Drink we did and drink we do, and no doubt, drink we will!

RED BEANS AND RICE:
New Orleans' Traditional Monday Dish

Before getting into the red beans and rice dish, let's have a look at the individual components:

Rice

No main meal was ever complete to a Creole without rice in some form. Rice is to Louisiana what potatoes are to Idaho. Annual per capita rice consumption here is close to 100 pounds compared to six puny pounds nationally. Our infatuation with rice is deeply inbred. My father-in-law, Jerome Trasimond Mire, never began eating until he had been served rice, even if it had to be placed next to his potatoes.

We owe our deep gratitude to a Sicilian immigrant named Angelo Sacola, known today as the father of the Louisiana rice industry. When he arrived in the Crescent City in 1849 at age 18, all rice consumed in our area came from South Carolina, the principal state producing rice in North America. At that time nearby Plaquemines Parish (county) was producing only 30,000 pounds per year, which did not satisfy the demands of the New Orleans area, much less that of Louisiana.

Upon arriving, Angelo surveyed the terrain and was pleased with what he found. With the cultivation of new seeds in the rich alluvial land and rotation of his crops, he and other Louisiana growers were soon able to produce over one million hundred weight sacks annually. Angelo's rice was responsible for making many Louisianians wealthy in a very short span of time.

He was also first to introduce steam-powered rice mills and thrashing machines. Before he finished building his empire his rice mill in New Orleans was the largest in the United States.

Angelo was also a humanitarian. He had read much about famine throughout the world and in his small way made a major contribution to alleviating hunger by sending seeds to international agricultural fairs. In so doing he encouraged rice growing worldwide and was honored with gold medals from nations whose populations were literally starving. Angelo was a great man in New Orleans but in foreign countries where people had never seen him he was looked upon as a savior.

Beans

The tradition of eating beans in New Orleans was introduced during the Spanish administration. Many of the Spanish leaders who came to New Orleans to serve as administrators brought along Cuban aides. In Cuba the tradition of eating beans had long been observed, and the Cubans coming to New Orleans kept their eating preferences, which were soon intermingled with other local eating habits. Thus, beans and rice became a traditional New Orleans food.

Red Beans and Rice

And now for the marriage made not in heaven but in the heaven on earth: New Orleans. Someone, and I'm sure we will never find out just who, mixed rice and beans together. The rare combination led ultimately to this traditional New Orleans delight which is eaten by more local families than any other single dish.

It became the practice to serve red beans and rice on Mondays for two reasons:

First, Monday was customarily washday in New Orleans. The time-consuming job would not permit the woman of the house to stand at the stove and stir, as was necessary for so many dishes. Red beans were cooked on a slow fire for as long as five or six hours. Secondly, meat was consumed at few meals during the week but was almost always a part of the Sunday dinner. Any meat left over from the Sunday meal could be added to the red beans to enhance the flavor.

There are literally hundreds of ways to prepare red beans and rice and every family has its own favorite recipe, but the results are like love: some great; all good.

If one were to ask which city is noted as bean city perhaps 99 percent would say "Boston." Statistics, on the other hand, show that 50 plus tons of red beans and rice are consumed weekly in New Orleans, thereby exceeding by far per capita consumption in any other city in the United States, including Boston.

It is ironic that the red kidney bean, which is used, is not even grown in the state of Louisiana. In fact, the seed for the red bean is produced in California, shipped to upstate New York for planting, and upon harvesting shipped back to this general area to be consumed in massive quantities.

One major problem with beans is that they tend to create intestinal gas. But it is claimed that the people of New Orleans have learned to solve that problem by cooking the beans upside down thereby giving one the hiccups.

The price of red beans and rice is considered an outstanding bargain, the taste is delicious and the nutritional value for the cost is unrivaled. For those reasons, in years gone by the New Orleans School Board adopted an ordinance whereby red beans and rice, because of their nutritional and brain-stimulating qualities, were required to be served at least twice a week to school children.

City-wide the statistics are staggering:

It is estimated that 600,000 plates of the dish are served weekly in the metropolitan New Orleans area. To get a count on the number of restaurants in New Orleans which serve this repast on Mondays, I let my fingers do the walking. The first 100 restaurants listed in the yellow pages all served this staple delicacy.

A plate of red beans and rice can be enjoyed either at the swanky Boston Club or purchased from the corner greasy spoon. Price will range anywhere from $1.50 to $8.00 with the difference only in the surroundings. It is true that not every visitor to our city likes the New Orleans specialty to the extent that Orleanians do. But 600,000 plates weekly of any dish is testimony to its popularity.

To the Italians and the Cubans who made this sumptuous repast possible we owe a lasting debt of gratitude. Hiccup!

"Guide to Excellent Restaurants"

New Orleanians not only rate their favorite restaurants with the discernment and conviction of professional critics, they also argue vehemently about them. Eating in our city is not only an art, it is an obsession. Visitors, however, are bombarded with such an array of excellence, selection of a restaurant can be perplexing. Newcomers especially are lacking the advantages of experience and the on-going public forum.

Usually, I recommend to a group, or a couple, that its mem-

bers must first establish a concensus on what the majority feel like
eating: veal, fish, fowl, seafood, beef, soul food, elegant French
fare, New Orleans-Italian, New Orleans-Indigeneous, Louisiana
Creole, modified Continental . . . the possibilities are endless.

With fish and shellfish so abundant from the Gulf, the Mississippi Sound, Lake Pontchartrain, estuarian waters and marshes,
the emphasis in my recommendations weigh heavily toward Neptune's treasures. Since most guests of our city will be living in the
French Quarter or Central Business District, I would like to sug-
gest a variety of eating establishments either within easy walking
distance or accessible by taxi or the St. Charles Streetcar Line. A
few will require private transportation, but to leave them out would
be remiss. Here goes:

At *ANTOINE'S* (713 St. Louis), I like to make a meal of hors
d'oeuvres—Crawfish Cardinal, Crabmeat Ravigot; several varieties of baked oysters on the half shell, notable among which are the
Rockefellers which were invented here; and Shrimp Remoulade to
name a few memorable delicacies. If your appetite is not satiated,
the beef, trout and Pompano (cooked in a paper bag) are excellent.
Make reservations and, above all, try to convince the maitre d' to
seat you in one of the back rooms away from the bland "tourist"
room up front which is totally devoid of conducive atmosphere.

ARNAUD'S (813 Bienville). The Trout Meuniere is, in my
opinion, unexcelled. Shrimp Arnaud is a superior appetizer and
cup custard, a light and rewarding dessert. Refurbished in 1979,
the restaurant dates back to 1917 when it was opened by Count Arnaud Cazenave.

BEGUE'S (300 Bourbon St., Royal Sonesta Hotel) noonday
buffet, varying from seafood to plantation to Creole dishes, is a
sharp contrast to the formal haute cuisine of the evening. The
French chef is high on his Royal Crawfish (tiny fresh water lobster), fresh vegetables and Floating Islands for dessert. I am, too.
Dress up for an elegant evening.

THE BON TON (401 Magazine) is a seafood-lover's dream
with its super crawfish (fried, etouffée, bisque) and a splash of crab
and shrimp entrees. The Red Fish Bon Ton, topped with lump
crabmeat, will tempt inlanders to move South. For dessert, don't
miss the bread pudding which is escorted by whiskey sauce.

To locals and visitors alike, *BRENNAN'S* (417 Royal Street) is synonymous with breakfast . . . not the early morning variety with scrambled eggs, bacon and juice. This is a brunchy feast with milk punch followed by fancy Eggs Benedict, Sardou, Hussard or St. Charles. How the lowly hen can be a party to such creations is beyond me.

For the hearty appetite, a wide range of fish temptations, (such as Red Fish Perez), will satisfy while entertaining the taste buds. Reservations are advised, and plan to spend a few minutes in the banana-treed courtyard enjoying the lush beauty and punch.

THE CARIBBEAN ROOM (2031 St. Charles Ave., Pontchartrain Hotel) invites you to dine as the wealthy aristocrats of the nineteenth century did. The finest cuisine will tease you with epicurean delights such as Trout Veronique, Shrimp Saki, Crabmeat Remick. The Mile High Pie would make Denverites blush.

Away from home for too long? Is your body craving home cooking . . . fresh veggies, corn bread, soul food? CHEZ HELENE'S (1540 N. Robertson Street) can be the right prescription for your condition. Southern-fried chicken, potato salad, red beans and rice, turnips, mustard greens, cabbage—the menu is clearly Creole. The small restaurant should win awards for its bread pudding. You will walk out a new person, ready to return to rich French foods and contemplating a delayed departure from the Crescent City.

CHRISTIANS (3835 Iberville) is located in a Lutheran Church building painted pink and trimmed in white. The church pews are used for seating and collection baskets are used as decorations on the walls between the stained glass windows. The unique atmosphere complements the triumphant flavors of the Oyster Chowder, Fish Bisque, Crab Meat Ravigotte and Red Fish au Poivre Bert. Chocolate Mousse tops off a unique dining experience in a unique atmosphere.

Upon leaving after a most pleasant evening I heard a solemn voice above say, "Bless You My Son" and I thought to myself, "I already have been."

COMMANDER'S PALACE (1403 Washington Avenue), a short ride on the streetcar along one of America's most beautiful avenues, offers the finest treasures from America's Gulf waters: Speckled Trout, Red Fish, soft-shell crab. Instead of a topping of almonds, Commander's prefers to lace its trout with Louisiana's fattest pecans. The Crabmeat Imperial is nothing short of fabulous, and the praline parfait will leave you defenseless. Ask for a table upstairs next to the giant live oak.

DELMONICO (1300 St. Charles) prepares French food with leanings toward the Creole. Dating back to 1895, the restaurant offers: Chicken Cordon Bleu, Snapper topped with crabmeat, sautéed calves liver, Trout Delmonico—all adorned with tasty fresh vegetables—to satisfy the most selective palate. Turtle soup, bathed in sherry, is a house specialty.

GALATOIRE'S (209 Bourbon, away from the skin games of the notorious street) is traditionally one of the highest-rated restaurants in this city of gourmets. The long daily and nightly lines of patient enthusiasts are testimony to the esteem with which this world-renowned establishment is regarded. A family enterprise, Galatoire's presents the best in salads (hearts of Romain and onions is my favorite). Exciting entrées like Pompano (cooked in a paper bag) or the same delectable fish cooked a la almondine, will not soon be forgotten. Oysters en brochette will fill and satisfy without leaving a stuffed feeling. Mirrored walls and bouncing light does not make a favorite atmosphere, but the food overshadows any distractions. Get in line early. You won't be disappointed.

K-PAUL'S (416 Chartres St.) is the rage in Louisiana Cajun cuisine. And proprietor Paul Prudhomme, the likeable, proud, talented Acadian, is the darling of culinary circles at home and nationally. A descendant of deposed Canadian French who came to Louisiana in the middle of the eighteenth century, rotund Paul has left leading French chefs in his wake during the last dozen or so years. (He was selected to cook for the Economic Conference at Camp David.)

Paul is a stickler for freshness, for fine-tuned balance in seasoning and for serving food immediately after it is cooked. Gumbo, fish dishes, crawfish tails (he fries them and calls them Louisiana Popcorn) are serendipity supreme. Like Galatoire's, K-Paul's will not accept reservations, so you can expect a line. However, because the place seats patrons European-style at any available chair, the wait is not usually a long one. And you meet the most interesting people!

LeRUTH'S (636 Franklin, across the River in Gretna) has repeatedly scored 3, 4, 5 stars from several respected national and international rating services, and justly so. Crabmeat St. Francis and Crawfish Cardinal are favorites, but almost every entrée is a pinnacle in the dining experience. Flounder, pompano, oysters, trout, frog legs—all are enhanced with subtle flavors through creative seasoning. Bread and ice cream are made in-house and the difference testifies to quality standards. Magnifique!

LOUIS XVI (829 Toulouse St., Marie Antoinette Hotel) is a stop to consider. If you hail from the Northeast and miss your fresh Maine lobster, this is your opportunity to compare. Expect to be elated. The filet mignon with bernaise sauce will make you forget that mid-Western beef. If the sauce frightens you, ask to have it on the side. Veal lovers will revel in the sumptuous presentations. Caramel custard and mousse get my vote for titilating desserts.

When presidents come to New Orleans they go to *PASCAL'S MANALE* (1838 Napoleon), not because of its ambience but because of its fame as a national-class New Orleans-Italian eating place. For presidents and others, there's one dish on the menu that makes the trip more than worthwhile. That's Manale's Barbecued Shrimp. Dress casually; you have to remove the shrimp shells yourself, but it's not an ordeal. Bibs, hand towels and finger bowls are provided. Juices from this heavenly concoction, sopped with warm French bread, will make you think you died and went to New Orleans. Trust me.

If the press of urbanity is weighing on you, and you have a car, why not take a short trip out of the hustle and bustle to *MAYER'S OLD EUROPE*, located across beautiful Lake Pontchartrain in Slidell (2998 Pontchartrain Drive). Let proprietor and chef George Mayer introduce you to unforgetable specialties. Trout Imperial is a marriage made in heaven between Speckled Trout and backfin lump crabmeat; Fettucini Alfredo, as a side dish to delicious paneed veal, is the best I've had anywhere, and his roast duckling with Madiera sauce is presented by the impresario as only the Europeans can. Located in a lovely restored home, space is at a premium; therefore, reservations are in order (1-649-1426). Say hello to wife, Carolyn . . . she's the spirit behind the successful operation.

THE RIB ROOM (621 St. Louis St., Royal Orleans Hotel) is perfect for those "up to here" with fish and crustacean repasts. Prime, aged, tender, flavorful rib of beef, partaken in this magnif-

icent old English decor is sure to suit the most discriminating meat
enthusiast. The onion soup is cooked to order and outstanding. For
anyone hooked on treasures from the deep, try some of the crabmeat dishes. The coffee with chickory is delightful.

The above are but a few of the dens of dining pleasure in and
around our fair city. There are dozens of others like Steven and
Martin for outstanding seafood (located between Louisiana and
Napoleon on St. Charles), Sazerac, La Riviera, Winston's, Versailles, Berdou's, The Andrew Jackson, Broussard's and hundreds
of neighborhood restaurants that would rival the best in any city
in America and abroad, including San Francisco and Paris.

But don't take my word for it. Take the trip to excellence, and
be prepared for a grand surprise. After all, dozens of nationalities
have contributed to this unique cuisine. WARNING: The food you
return to may never taste the same.

CHAPTER TWO

Cemeteries

 Cemetery is a Greek word meaning "to lie down." In early New Orleans, if you dug a six-foot hole you would soon have a hole with up to 5 feet 11¾ inches of water because of the city's high water table and below sea-level elevation. As a result, a coffin would float in the grave; it literally had to be emersed. In fact, a coffin placed in a freshly dug grave floated on top until men forced it with long wooden poles to settle on the bottom. To eliminate this agonizing sight, large holes were bored into the bottoms of coffins so water could enter quickly and force the coffin to sink without delay.

Imagine listening to the coffin of a loved one, gurgling, gurgling, gurgling, as it sank to its rest. This painful ordeal led to the practice of building tombs above ground. Hence the term "the cities of the dead," which has been used in South Louisiana to describe cemeteries.

A humorist said, "Death is simply nature's way of telling us to slow down." And a very famous writer, upon visiting New Orleans, said,

> "You can tell a great deal about a community by the way they honor their dead, and without meeting any of the people of New Orleans yet, I can tell you I know I'm going to like them, for very few cities that I have visited throughout the world honor the dead as they do here in New Orleans."

New Orleans' cemeteries have been the sites of a multitude of unusual happenings and no doubt a source of fascination for the visitors to our city. In 1980 a vice-president of Neiman-Marcus of Houston, Texas, chose Lafayette Cemetery on Washington Avenue as the site for his wedding. The date was Friday, the 13th of June.

A chartered flight from Houston brought the bride, groom and guests, all dressed in black. Four black limosines took the wedding party to Lafayette Cemetery. The ceremony was held in one of the aisles of the cemetery, while a lone trumpet played "Summertime." The bride and groom, both married previously, told the graveyard superintendent they had come to bury the past and get married at the same time.

CITY'S FIRST CEMETERY

One of the first problems faced in New Orleans was what to do with the first person who died. The only high ground in the city was along the river, a ridge created from silt in the annual overflow of the mighty Mississippi. This area was used as a cemetery for a while, but city leaders soon realized that digging could weaken what little flood protection the city had. Therefore, an ordinance forbidding burial there was enacted.

In 1721 Adrian dePauger, Royal Military Engineer, arrived to lay out the streets of the new town. A cemetery was designated on the outskirts of the little settlement. An early plan dated May 20, 1725 shows it as extending along the upper side of St. Peter Street between streets now known as Burgundy and Rampart. At the time the cemetery was established the streets extended from the river to Dauphine Street. When the first effort to fortify the city was made after the Indian massacre of the French at Natchez in 1729, a ditch serving as a moat was located along the street. This placed the cemetery outside the moat and it was reached only by a twisting road from the end of Orleans Street.

Although Cabildo records of November 14, 1800 indicate an earlier cemetery was located in New Orleans, no other records confirm this. So the St. Peter Street Cemetery is considered the first cemetery in the city. Not all New Orleans' people were buried in the cemetery. For example, Adrian dePauger died in June of 1726 and was buried in the foundation beneath an uncompleted church (the Church of St. Louis) which he had designed. In 1769 Lester St. Martin, a major financial contributor to the church, was buried within the edifice. He must have been very important; records tell us that for the occasion the church was draped in black and lighted by 272 candles. Other prominent business, political, and spiritual leaders have been buried within the walls of the church of St. Louis, now called St. Louis Cathedral.

In 1798 the most influential man in Louisiana, Don Andrès Almonaster y Roxas, died. Since he was the man who completely rebuilt the city of New Orleans after the great fire of 1788, it was only natural that he be buried inside the Cathedral.

In 1799 Louisiana Governor Manuel Gayuso deLemos became the only colonial governor to be buried within Louisiana, and he is also buried in St. Louis Cathedral. A total of nine archbishops of New Orleans are buried in the structure. The last burial within the walls of the Cathedral was that of Archbishop Rummel in 1964.

Residents of lesser ranks, however, were buried in the cemetery on the outskirts of town. As the city expanded people began building homes around the cemetery. Soon they began complaining to political leaders about the unpleasantness of having to sit on the front stoop or porch in the evening while being confronted with the eerie sight of a cemetery. Of course in the eighteenth century there were no electric fans or air conditioners. One had no choice but to sit outdoors to catch the slightest murmur of a breeze.

Political leaders in 1742 were quick to respond to the agitation of the complainants. It was decided that a five-foot brick wall would solve the problem. Wealthy citizens donated the brick and mortar and the poor folks furnished the labor. The wall was ceremoniously dedicated on All Saints Day in 1743. A large wooden cross was erected in the center of the burial ground. People came to the dedication with flowers for the deceased just as was the custom on All Saints Day throughout Europe. This is believed to be the first celebration and observance of the tradition in Louisiana.

Before the advent of Christianity, pagans for the most part worshipped nature as their god. Their two big celebrations were the festival of life and the festival of death, celebrated in observance of the birth (Spring) of nature and its death (Winter). The Catholic Church borrowed from this idea, and in place of nature, honored the festival of life as Easter (the resurrection of Christ into Heaven) and the festival of death (All Saints Day) to commemorate the memory of the deceased.

For 70 years under French and Spanish rule, the city continued to grow and its population multiplied. Gradually, the St. Peter Street Cemetery began to fill up. By the year 1788 it was filled to capacity. That year has the distinction of being the worst, in terms of calamity, in the city's illustrious history. To begin with, the mighty Mississippi overflowed and the city was completely inundated.

On March 21, 1788, Good Friday proved not to be such a good Friday after all, as the city's worst fire burned 856 houses to the ground. Four-fifths of the city that was there one day was gone the next. If that wasn't tragic enough, during the same year the city was visited by serious epidemics that took sizable tolls on the population.

The completely-filled cemetery had to be covered with lime to prevent a serious outbreak of pestilence. The cemetery was ordered closed and a new one further from the city's population was to be established.

The square that was once occupied by the city's first cemetery is today a residential square for the living, and not as once called, a "city of the dead."

The city's oldest surviving cemetery, St. Louis No. 1, was approved by a Royal Decree on August 14, 1789. At the same time a royal edict decreed that the old St. Peter Street Cemetery was to be used as a site for the construction of houses. In spite of this fiat burial continued for several years in the St. Peter Street Cemetery, even after St. Louis No. 1 was operative. People apparently considered it ridiculous to go to another cemetery that was much farther away. Besides, they didn't like the new cemetery. Someone jokingly said St. Louis No. 1 was laid out by a drunken sailor. Survivors went in, turned and twisted around already existing tombs and simply picked an open spot. The narrow paths in the cemetery had little grass and only an occasional shrub or palm. Tombs were made of brick because there was no natural stone near New Orleans. The soft red brick was the least expensive building material at hand but it deteriorated quickly because of the elements. Consequently it became necessary, and then became the custom,

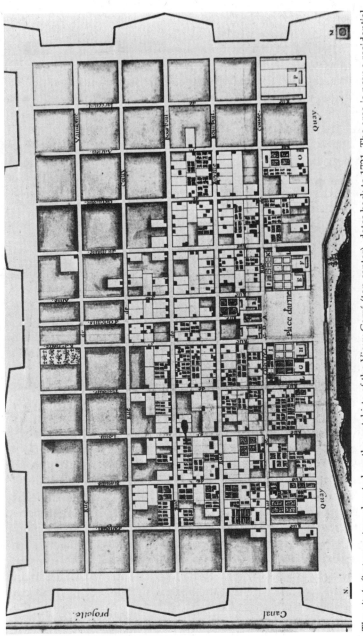

The city's first cemetery, located on the outskirts of the Vieux Carré (top center), dates back to 1721. The area is now a residential neighborhood. (The Historic New Orleans Collection)

to plaster the soft red brick and paint the plaster white as a symbol of purity.

After the Louisiana Purchase in 1803 a burial site for non-Catholics was established. In 1805 a small burial ground at the rear of the cemetery (like the old segregated policy of blacks in the rear of the bus) was dedicated to non-Catholic burial. In the rear of the Protestant section there was a graveyard for Negroes. So, there were three classes of burials in one cemetery.

St. Louis No. 1 is located now on Basin Street. Originally the cemetery extended two blocks closer to the River (almost to Rampart Street), but was cut in two in 1908 when the Southern Railroad tracks came through what is now called Basin Street to reach the Southern Railroad Terminal Station on Canal and Basin Streets.

The famous cemetery is crowded with the graves of historical figures. It has had its share of misfortune, like its total flooding in 1816 from a break in the levee at the Macarty Plantation. This disaster dictated a brief closing of the city's only cemetery with all bodies buried temporarily on the West Bank of the River.

St. Louis has also had its moments of humor. The two wives of the state's first governor, William C. C. Claiborne, are buried in St. Louis No. 1 with Claiborne's brother-in-law between them. Why William C. C. Claiborne is buried in another cemetery across town is still not known.

Also unique is the fact that even the cemetery's walls have been used for burial. Since high ground was already at a premium, two parallel cemetery walls were built approximately 12 feet high and eight feet apart. Four levels of crypts were available between the full length of the walls. These old wall burial places were called, and are still known as "wall-ovens," because they looked like ovens for baking bread.

The older wall-ovens were of brick. To get the necessary strength for the four different levels, curved arches were designed to provide the structural strength for coffin openings. The extreme depth of the tombs made it possible to move the remains of the bodies to the back of the tomb, to a lower shelf or crypt. According to Louisiana law, a sealed tomb could not be opened for a year and a day, the reason being that the body would be well past the state of spreading disease.

Considering the fact that New Orleans is semi-tropical, the constant pounding of the summer sun on an above-ground tomb literally turned it into a crematory. After one year and one day the coffins, usually made of pine, were well on their way to decomposition, and only the large bones of skeletons were in evidence.

Today, 193 years after the formal dedication of St. Louis No. 1 Cemetery, the poor souls in the bottom vaults in the wall-ovens are more than half below ground because of the weight of the walls on poor foundations. Of course, the parties involved have few complaints.

In early days poor families were required to make their own coffins. Sextons of the cemeteries sold used coffin hardware and materials at the gates of all the cemeteries to earn a few extra nickels. With a few chickens and ducks, they also kept goats in the cemeteries to serve as grass cutters and milk producers.

St. Louis No. 1 also was the first cemetery in New Orleans with vaults to serve the deceased who belonged to benevolent societies. These societies were the forerunners of the insurance companies and were instituted by the Spanish and later copied by the French, Portuguese and other nationalities.

The most striking of the society tombs in St. Louis No. 1 is the Italian Mutual Benevolent Society tomb, founded in 1848 by Joseph A. Barelli, a prominent New Orleanian.

The Baroque marble circular tomb, designed by noted Italian architect Pietro Gualdi, contains 241 vaults. A receptacle in its basement is closed off by an iron door. The monument is completely surrounded by a beautifully-designed iron fence. At the very top of the monument is a female figure holding a cross. Two niches, one with a large statue representing "Italia" and the other with a statue of a woman representing "Charity," add personality to the tomb.

This magnificent society tomb was dedicated with pomp and ceremony in 1857. Its construction cost of $40,000 was a sizable sum at the time. The first person to be buried in it was Pietro Gualdi, the architect, and the second was Joseph A. Barelli, the president and founder of the society; hence the nickname for the monument immediately became the "Hex Tomb." The sobriquet has stuck until today.

Although it is impossible to name all of the famous and infamous people who have been buried in St. Louis No. 1, here are a few:

Etienne Boré, New Orleans' first-appointed Mayor and the first man to granulate sugar; his grandson, Louisiana's first historian, Charles Gayarré.

Daniel Clark, wealthy Irish merchant and one of the city's most colorful characters; his illegitimate daughter, Myra Clark Gaines.

Paul Morphy, the first world chess champion from North America. (The home of Paul Morphy is now a famous restaurant in New Orleans called Brennan's.)

Bernard deMarigny, America's first millionaire playboy and the man who introduced dice to North America.

Marie Laveau, New Orleans' most notorious voodoo queen, and some say, the last well-known witch of North America.

Pierre Derbigny, the governor of Louisiana who drew up the state's civil code. (Derbigny died of an accident on September 25, 1829, as a result of being thrown from his carriage by runaway horses belonging to none other than Marie Laveau.)

It is worth the time to visit St. Louis No. 1, one of the most interesting cemeteries to be found anywhere.

THE BURYING CHURCH

Because the original St. Louis Cathedral (called the Church of St. Louis before its dedication as a cathedral in 1794) was the first church building in New Orleans, and because of its location in the center of the French Quarter, people just assume the current building is the oldest church building in New Orleans. But it is not. The *present* structure was built by a contract signed on March 12, 1849 and completed in 1850 at a total cost of $96,000. The builder was an Irish contractor named John Patrick Kirwan.

In 1825 Père Antoine, pastor of the cathedral, purchased a piece of land, where the Church of Our Lady of Guadalupe was located, for the sum of $425. It was ideally located for funerals as it was adjacent to the St. Louis No. 1 Cemetery. On October 10, 1826, Père Antoine held a ground breaking ceremony, and in 1827 the $14,000 church was completed . . . some 23 years before the present structure of St. Louis Cathedral was completed.

The first funeral was held on November 1, All Saints Day, for Dr. Joseph Elbram. Originally called the mortuary chapel, it didn't take long for it to serve the purpose for which it was built: burial Masses. In the 1830s New Orleans was visited by "Bronze John" (yellow fever). In fear of spreading the epidemics, burials from the cathedral were discontinued.

Inside the mortuary chapel there were no pews or altar. In the center of the room, a raised platform on which the coffins were placed was surrounded by 12 huge candles "as tall as a ship's mast." When a coffin was brought in it was placed upon the platform and the mourners would stand around, each holding a small candle. All would pray in silence while waiting for the priest to perform the burial ceremony. After the burial-Mass services were completed two aisles were formed by the people holding the candles. While the casket was carried out to the front of the church the priest and the altar boys went out of the back and directly into the cemetery. The people, the hearse and the body first went on parade through the French Quarter before going to the cemetery. In the early days of New Orleans it was unheard of to go directly from church to cemetery.

The original purpose of the church as a mortuary chapel was achieved, but conditions changed and the church had to change with the times.

In 1865, following the end of the Civil War, the church was the favorite meeting place of Confederate soldiers and their Confederate chaplain, Father Turgis, who was quite proficient in tending to their needs. A large number of Italian immigrants arrived in the city in 1873, and the church then became the Italian church of St. Anthony. In 1921 the Oblate Fathers made their appearance and became administrators of the Church, again referred to as Our Lady of Guadalupe. In 1935 we see the beginning of the devotion of St. Jude, the patron of difficult and impossible cases, which is still being held therein. The place of worship became the official chapel of the New Orleans Police and Fire Department in 1953, with Father Peter Rogers serving as both police and fire chaplain, positions held by Oblate Fathers since 1931.

To survive, churches, like people, must adjust to change. The Church of Our Lady of Guadalupe, the oldest church building in New Orleans, is aptly called "the church that would not die."

BRONZE JOHN AND
OTHER UNWELCOME KILLERS

Today New Orleans has a total of 41 cemeteries within its city limits. Many of their tenants were struck down during periodic visits of uninvited killers. The biggest killer of all was yellow fever.

In only one century yellow fever alone caused more than 50,000 deaths and afflicted more than a half million people in the south. This dreaded disease was called "Bronze John" because of the skin color of its victims.

Beginning in 1796 and proceeding into the twentieth century, the city suffered recurrent attacks of yellow fever. Because of the high mortality rate, an 1832 law required burial within 24 hours of death or a $100 fine was imposed. During a one-month period 300 people were dying each day from this terrible, agonizing disease. Thousands upon thousands died that year.

Dr. Theodore Clapp, in his autobiographical sketches and recollections during his 35 years of residence in New Orleans, wrote

> Many persons even of fortune and popularity died in their beds without aid, unnoticed and unknown and lay there for days unburied. In almost every house might be seen the sick, the dying and the dead. All the stores, banks and places of business were closed. There were no means, no instruments for carrying on the ordinary affairs of business, for all the drays, carts, carriages, hand and common wheelbarrows, as well as hearses were employed in the transportation of corpses instead of cotton, sugar and passengers. Words cannot describe my sensation when I first beheld the awful sight of carts driven to the graveyard and there upturned and their contents discharged as so many loads of lumber or offal, without a single mark of mourning or respect, because the exigency made it impossible.
>
> Often I was kept in the burying grounds for hours in succession by the incessant unintermitting arrival of corpses over whom I was requested to perform a short service. One day, I did not leave the cemetery until 9 o'clock at night, until a last internment was made

by candlelight. Reaching my house faint, I found my family all sob-
bing and weeping, for they had concluded from my long absence
that I was certainly dead.

During the same epidemic, Roger Baudier wrote an article in
the Catholic Church newspaper in Louisiana describing the horrible sights that were seen during these terrible times:

> During the 1832-33 yellow fever-cholera epidemic, the portals
> of the mortuary chapel remained ajar from the break of day to late
> evening with endless processions of corpses. Disgraceful scenes took
> place at the chapel where families and undertakers wrangled and
> fought each other to bring bodies into the chapel for final rites of the
> church. Some unable to gain entrance went to the cemetery for burial
> without benefit of clergy.

During these terrible times it was difficult to find laborers to
dig the graves for all those who had died. Available diggers were
given large quantities of alcohol so that the stench of the dead
would not be overpowering. Bodies were brought to the cemetery
in loads and dumped into common graves. Mothers could be seen
bringing their children in small coffins carried on their heads.

Between 1718 and 1860, 23 yellow fever epidemics were recorded, with 1853 being by far the worst of them all. It was estimated that 12,000 New Orleanians died in that one year.

William L. Robinson, in his *Diary of a Samaritan*, wrote:

> By the tenth of August, the mortality had reached an appall-
> ing height. The whole city was a hospital. The streets were de-
> serted, save for the hasty pedestrians on errands of mercy. Normal
> sounds of rattling of an omnibus and the swing of the doctor's rig
> as either rapidly passed, were the only disturbing sounds. The nor-
> mal sounds of the coalman, the knife grinder and others' callings
> that enliven the thoroughfares were silenced by the fear of the dis-
> ease.
>
> The morning train of funerals crowded the road to the ceme-
> teries. It was an unbroken line of carriages and omnibuses for two-
> and-a-half miles. The city's commissary wagons and carts of the dif-
> ferent hospitals with their loads of eight or ten coffins each fell in
> with the cortage of citizens.

The most frustrating thing about fighting yellow fever was

that the people did not know what they were fighting. In igno-
rance of the cause of the disease, city fathers were fighting like men
trying to beat their own shadows. Employing unusual methods
they imposed the burning of tar on street corners in hopes that the
measure would drive away evil spirits. Citizens turned black and
became sick to their stomachs. Since burning tar did not work the
city resorted to firing cannons on street corners in hopes that this
would drive away the demons. This plan gave everyone a head-
ache but little else. People were still dying by the thousands, no
matter what the city fathers did. As a final resort they decided to
construct a room in which an extremely hot fire could be built. Pa-
tients were taken into the room and wrapped in blankets. When
the blankets dripped with perspiration saturation, sufferers were
dumped into cold water. If this process didn't cure them, the shock
surely must have killed some.

A solution was imminent! With the help of what had been
learned earlier by the Havana Yellow Fever Commission, New Orleans, under the guidance of the city's health officer Dr. Quitman
Kohnke, rolled up its sleeves to fight the now-discovered enemy,
the *Aedes Aegypti* mosquito. The tiny pesky insect was to be erad-
icated from the city as completely as humanly possible. Because of
the urgency of the matter and the vast amounts of water in the city
limits, city fathers asked the federal government to take charge of
the campaign to rid the city of the epidemic. The U.S. Public Health
Service and the Marine Hospital Service, under the leadership of
Dr. Joseph H. White, utilized the strategy outlined by Cuban doctor Walter Reed. With a virtual army of volunteers every house in
the city was checked and all possible breeding grounds were elim-
inated. All open gutters were salted down and 68,000 cisterns were
either screened or oiled (a thin film of oil on the surface precluded
mosquito breeding).

The 1905 death toll in New Orleans of 423 was the last recorded yellow fever epidemic. It is believed that had leaders acted
more quickly in doing the things necessary to eliminate the breeding grounds of the *Aedis Aegypti*, the city would not have recorded
any yellow fever deaths that year. But New Orleans has always
been noted for being slow to move. Usually the only fast move has
been the move to procrastinate, in fact, that particular laissez-faire

trait is still part of the makeup of New Orleanians. Who knows . . . a problem might be solved by time.

MACABRE HAPPENING IN POTTER'S FIELD

Like other cities in America, New Orleans has a pauper's field for the indigent.

In this unusual but true story, a worker went slightly overboard in carrying out his duties, according to the New Orleans *Bulletin* of May 29, 1875.

The headlines were shockers and instantly drew attention of many readers:

Buried Alive
Sickening tale of our hospital dead.
A man in the charity wagon revives.
He attempts to get out of his coffin.
The driver smothers him.
Full details and statement of witness.

The story accused the driver of the Charity Hospital wagon of *killing a dead man*. And yes, there was a witness to the murder of the purported dead man. The witness, C. H. Beggs, testified that he saw the incident and was quoted by the newspaper:

The driver lifted out a coffin and was about to deposit it in the hole prepared for it, when the occupant of the coffin kicked off the lid and cried, 'For God sakes, do not bury me alive.' The driver picked up a brick and crying, 'You blank, blank, I have a doctor's certificate that you are dead, and I'm going to bury you'. He then struck the man and stunning him or killing him, proceeded with the burial.

The newspaper turned whatever information it collected over to the New Orleans Police Department, which accepted it coolly and did not seem to think it worth investigating. In a subtle way the newspaper advised the Police Department that a reporter would be assigned full-time to get to the bottom of the murder or incident, whatever it turned out to be.

In self defense the police arrested the driver and proceeded to follow up on the case. The dead man, who was said to have been killed by the driver, was a 19-year-old black youth named George Banks who was in Charity Hospital as a smallpox victim. It was said that the driver, Jimmy Connors, was extremely willing but possibly not all there mentally. Some said he had "a rattling between the ears." The sexton of the cemetery, a Mr. Schwartz, knew Jim well and came to his defense. He said Jim was a good-hearted man and when Jim turned the body over to him the man was truly dead. He said he thought the pine coffin had fallen apart from the jolting of the wagon over the cobblestone streets.

Statements taken by the police from various eyewitnesses were all contradictory.

Mary Thompson said, "I saw a man in that coffin; he was alive. The driver picked up a baby's coffin that was also in the wagon and put it on top of him and sat on it."

Rosa Johnson stated, "I saw the arms of the man raised. I knew he was alive. The driver put a pillow over his head and smothered him."

William Harrison recalled, "I looked into the coffin, the man was breathing and the driver had dropped a big cobblestone on his chest."

Mrs. Louise Weber remembered, "The grave digger told me the driver was a funny kind of man, and he did it all as a joke."

With all of these conflicting views, the police were now totally confused, and according to the *Bulletin*, the case was brought to an end with no satisfactory conclusion.

The only evidence was that poor George Banks was buried. And we assume and hope he was buried dead. As to whether he died from smallpox, from being smothered by a pillow, crushed by a big cobblestone or a baby's coffin, we will never know. What we do know is that Jimmy Connors did take his job seriously . . . or did he?

FUNERAL OF C. C. W.—
WITH NO BODIES

The year 1852 has to go down as the year of the most spectacular funeral ever held in New Orleans.

None of the deceased were Orleanians . . . not even Louisianians.

The three men were from Kentucky, South Carolina and Massachusetts. Their names were Henry Clay, Daniel Webster and John Calhoun, three great American statesmen and orators of the nineteenth century. Over a two-year period each departed this earth.

On October 24, 1852, the *Times Picayune* ran an extra notifying its readers of the sad news of the death of the last to expire, Daniel Webster. A committee was formed to pay tribute to this great statesman, but when it met the names of Clay and Calhoun were proposed also. The idea of honoring the three men simultaneously met with complete approval. The gears were put into mesh for the colossal funeral services with the date set for December 9, 1852. A lengthy and most impressive program was printed for mass distribution. Merchants were asked to close their businesses and buildings were to be draped in mourning. Flags all over town and on all ships in the harbor were to be flown at half mast. Every club and military organization was invited to attend. Invitations were sent to the governor, to the mayors of all the cities in the state and to all foreign consuls.

The big day arrived. At 11:00 A.M. on December 9, 1852, the Grand Marshall gave the signal, and with a muffled boom of cannons at measured intervals and the tolling of church bells, the funeral procession began. The principal attraction was the funeral car pulled by six gray horses. It was 11 feet long and 16 feet high, and covered with black velvet with the names of Clay, Webster and Calhoun written thereon in silver letters. In each corner were black plumes. Two bronze eagles graced each side of the car and in its center, covered by a canopy, were three urns bearing the initials of the illustrious men.

Pallbearers, numbering 30, one for each state of the Union, marched in single file alongside the car. Some 5,000 participants in the funeral, all wearing proper mourning attire, took one-and-a-half hours to pass a given spot. The crowd was as big as had ever been seen in a New Orleans funeral. Not only were the people throughout the streets, but they were hanging from every window of every building. Some even stood on rooftops.

The parade ended at Lafayette Square where a mammoth, 60-foot-high simulated-marble cenotaph was erected to accept the urns. After they were taken from the wagon to the altar an impressive death-like stillness prevailed while the Rev. Mr. Walker gave a brief benediction. Dismissed by the Grand Marshall, the crowd dispersed from the square to the sounds of joyful music. Mourners headed for three locations shown in the program where three different eulogies were given.

Later that evening Lafayette Square presented a strange spectacle. It was lighted by torches arranged in the shape of a cross. The night was black and windy, and the ghostly glare of lights on the cenotaph created an impressive, awesome and eerie scene.

Further recognition was to be given to these men as statues of all three were to be placed on the major intersections on Canal Street.

On April 12, 1860, the citizens of New Orleans honored Henry Clay by dedicating a 14-foot statue of this American statesman at the corner of Canal and St. Charles/Royal streets. The largest float ever involved in a New Orleans parade was used at this ceremony. A 30-ton ship, with sails unfurled, was taken from the Mississippi River and put on a special undercarriage to be pulled down Canal Street.

Unfortunately, because of traditional New Orleans procrastination, statues of the other two men never materialized. And the statue of Henry Clay, dedicated on April 12, 1860, was removed in 1900 because it was considered a hindrance to growing traffic. It was placed in Lafayette Square, which ironically also has statues of John McDonogh and Benjamin Franklin, but no statue of General Lafayette.

These three great statesmen are still honored with street names. Calhoun, Clay, and Webster run from the river to the lake.

ODD FELLOWS REST

The secret benevolent society called the Independent Order of Odd Fellows began in New Orleans in 1831. By 1840 a sizable membership had been enrolled so that in 1847 sufficient funds were available for the society to purchase land to be used as a cemetery. Costing $700, a triangular tract between Canal Street and Metairie Road (now City Park Avenue) and St. Patrick Cemetery was purchased. Members of the Old Fellows were pleased with their purchase; the land was high and was one of the few places in the city to stay dry during the serious flooding of 1849.

Unlike old St. Louis No. 1 Cemetery, Odd Fellows Rest had a well-organized design with "wall ovens" on two sides of the triangular piece of land. To honor some of its members walks were laid out and named for members who had served as past grand masters in the State of Louisiana.

The dedication plans were discussed and great pomp and ceremony were planned for the dedication date on February 29, 1849. The plan called for a grand procession led by two circus band wagons; one from Stone and McCollum's Circus to be drawn by sixteen magnificent horses, and the second from the circus of S. P. Stickney, drawn by four horses. The band wagons were followed by a funeral "car."

Large and grand, the funeral car carried the remains of 16 deceased members of the organization gathered from various cemeteries throughout the city.

After leaving the *Place d'Arms* the procession traveled through Chartres, Royal, Canal, Esplanade, Camp and St. Joseph streets. Members then headed to the New Basin Canal where the Odd Fellows boarded 35 chartered omnibuses for the trip along the New Basin shell road to the site of the cemetery three miles away. At this point the procession stretched out for a mile. Leaders of the grand lodge did not go by way of the shell road, instead they made the trip by water after boarding passenger barges on the New Basin Canal that took them to within a short distance of their own cemetery.

Although the society is no longer active, the secret benevolent society of the Independent Order of Odd Fellows made a lasting impression on February 29, 1849.

COLONEL W. W. S. BLISS

Renowned Colonel W. W. S. Bliss (Fort Bliss, Texas, was named in his honor) was a veteran of the Mexican War, and consequently, a target of many Mexican bullets. Colonel Bliss, however, did not lose his life to a Mexican bullet but to a tiny bite from a mosquito in New Orleans in 1852. Bliss, unfortunately, became one of the statistics in the great yellow fever epidemic of that year and was buried in the city's first Protestant cemetery in New Orleans, the Girod Street Cemetery.

When the city drew plans for the new city hall complex in the
1950s the Girod Street Cemetery, which had fallen into terrible dis-
repair, had to be moved to make room for the proposed structure.
In 1957 the United States Army sent a team of experts to secure,
verify and convey the remains of Colonel W. W. S. Bliss to the fort
in Texas named in his honor. Henry Gondolfo, a local expert with
unequaled expertise in this field, was chosen to assist the United
States Army in its assignment.

The imposing Bliss monument was constructed of Quincy
granite. The column leading from the large base was broken and
covered with a shroud, symbolizing death before the expected time.

Gondolfo, after extensive research, advised the army brass
his studies indicated a heavy slate located below the monument
served as a protective shield between the monument and the cast-
iron coffin. When the army dug down four feet they reached the
slate just as Gondolfo had advised. Gondolfo said that on removal
of the slate they would find the cast-iron coffin in the shape of the
human body, like the old Egyptian coffins. He stated that there
would be a glass plate over the face area where they would be able
to see the face of Colonel Bliss. Records indicated that the body
would be without a coat and epaulettes on the shoulders. The space
in the coffin was so limited the coat and epaulettes had been removed to close it. Gondolfo then told them the body, before being
dressed in uniform, had been wrapped in a light gauze-like material that was to serve as a wick. Before the cast-iron coffin was
sealed airtight, arsenic had been poured into the heel portion of
the coffin. Over a period of time the arsenic had been absorbed by
the gauze to moisten the body and aid in its preservation, hopefully for eternity.

Gondolfo said he would stake his reputation on a prediction
that the body would be in almost perfect condition in spite of having been sealed for 105 years. Gondolfo then recommended that a
transparent plastic cover be made to replace the cast-iron cover immediately on its removal, thereby saving the body. The body could
then be shipped to Fort Bliss, Texas, and be put on display for pos-
terity.

When the slate was removed the cast-iron, body-shaped coffin with glass front in the face area was there, just as Gondolfo had
said it would be. The glass was cleaned off with a fresh cloth and

the face, with the exception of the tip of the nose where it touched the glass, was just like it had been in 1852.

Unfortunately, a "fly in the ointment" came in the form of military red tape. The commanding officer ordered the coffin brought to a local funeral home where, according to his orders, the top was removed (without a plastic replacement being made beforehand). The body was examined to be sure it was the remains of Colonel Bliss.

First, the trousers were cut to check the bones in the legs; next, the teeth were to be taken out and examined. But before all of the checking could be completed Colonel Bliss protested vehemently by emitting an unbelievable gaseous stench that was so unbearable it drove everyone from the funeral home. As one man said, it was as though a hundred skunks had fumigated the building with all of the windows and doors closed tightly. The body then started to deteriorate rather rapidly, and in a short time it was no longer recognizable. It is unfortunate that army red tape deprived us of seeing a great military leader just the way he looked when he drew his last breath in 1852.

It would be safe to bet that the breaths drawn by those in the funeral home that day would haunt their senses of smell for the balance of their lives.

Adios Colonel!

FAITH, HOPE, CHARITY AND MRS. MORIARTY

At what was once the main entrance of Metairie Cemetery one will find the largest monument in the cemetery and possibly the tallest, privately-owned monument anywhere in the United States. From Interstate 10, when crossing the Metairie Road overpass, you can't miss it because it stands out like a sore thumb—all 85 feet of it.

As the story goes, Daniel Moriarty, an Irish immigrant, worked hard and was a very successful businessman. His wife was much older than he, and Daniel was not as attentive to her as he could have been. Some go so far as to say that he was extermely unkind to her while she was alive. But he tried to make amends after she died in 1887.

Although Daniel was successful in commerce, he and his wife

One of the tallest privately-owned monuments in the United States is the Moriarty Monument located in Metairie Cemetery. (From the Buddy Stall Collection)

could never break into New Orleans society. They simply didn't have that good old New Orleans blue blood.

Daniel, having a silver tongue and the ability to get his ideas across, convinced a friend to design an impressive memorial. He ordered an overpowering monument with a huge granite shaft topped with a cross of the same material. Since Metairie was a cemetery where most of the blue bloods in New Orleans were buried, Daniel wanted his wife to look down her nose at those who had snubbed the Moriartys for so many years. The cross was to be so large a man would be able to stand under the arm. This he hoped would give his departed spouse great satisfaction.

Daniel told the sculptor he wanted four life-size statues to represent the four graces. When informed there were but three Graces—Faith, Hope and Charity—he insisted that there be four Graces anyway.

Daniel was successful in convincing a big out-of-state builder that this monument, in a city well-known for cemetery monuments, would bring him untold dollars. The final cost was $185,000. (Moriarty paid only a very small portion of that amount.)

Upon arrival of the monument it was discovered that no local drayage company had equipment large enough to transport it. A railroad spur from the main line had to be laid directly into the cemetery in order to make on-site delivery. The first erecting firm went bankrupt and a second contractor was hired. The monument, including the huge granite cross at the top of an eight-sided sphere, with the life-size statues of the "four Graces," was finally erected.

A circular sidewalk installed around the base of the monument consisted of stones from the various states throughout the country, each weighing eleven tons. When the walk was completed Mrs. Moriarty's remains were transferred from her original burial site to Metairie Cemetery.

As stated above, Mrs. Moriarty was much older than her husband, and in her will she stipulated that only the date of her death be shown. She didn't want to give anyone the satisfaction of knowing how much older she was than her spouse.

After the stone cutter inscribed the information given him by Moriarty he realized the date he'd carved was one day off the date he had been instructed to chisel on the monument. He approached Moriarty very tactfully and advised him that, apparently in his time of grief, he had made an understandable error, but the error could be corrected for the small sum of $2.50. Grunting, Moriarty said, "The hell with it, I've spent enough already."

After the remains of Mrs. Moriarty were placed under the monument Moriarty called the contractor back to the monument and advised him that the cross was crooked and he would not pay one cent until it was corrected. The second contractor went back to work, and like the first went bankrupt.

Moriarty moved to California for health reasons, and upon his death 36 years later was buried alongside his wife, Mary, under the highly controversial Moriarty monument.

When tour guides lead groups through Metairie Cemetery they point out the monument and tell the story as told above. The four life-size statues, they say, stand for faith, hope, charity and Mrs. Moriarty. But the truth is the fourth statue represents memories. And I must confess that Daniel Moriarty has given us a lot of entertaining memories in hearing and telling the story of his very controversial but magnificent monument to his neglected wife, Mary . . . the fourth grace.

CHAPTER THREE

*S*treets

Because New Orleans is a city with more territory below than above sea level, it naturally costs more to build and maintain streets here than in almost any other city in the United States. This is also the reason why New Orleans, per capita, has more unpaved streets than any other city of its size in America.

It is half-jokingly said that some of our streets have holes so big it would be cheaper to build bridges over them than to fill them.

In the early days of New Orleans, because it was practically surrounded by water, our city was literally called the "Isle of Orleans." Numerous drawings from the eighteenth century show French Quarter streets with wooden bridges from curb to curb so pedestrians could go from one "island" to the other.

In the French Quarter the words "Rue" and "Calle" are still used on street signs; these are, respectively, the French and Spanish words for "street." Unlike today, a great deal of thought went into the naming of streets in our city's formative years.

One who takes the time to study the history behind the naming of the streets of Old New Orleans will probably know more about the city's history than most of the natives. Like all aspects of New Orleans' heritage, the history behind the naming of some of our streets is quite entertaining, interesting and sometimes downright hilarious. This chapter will cover naming the first streets of

New Orleans, the widest main thoroughfare in the United States, the toughest and meanest street in the world and the city's first avenue and how it came about.

STREETS OF THE VIEUX CARRÉ

At the time of the establishment of New Orleans, the French were wallowing through a period of history without the leadership of a reigning king. Louis XIV had died at a less than propitious time, leaving behind a son too young to assume the reins of government.

Into the power vacuum moved Philip II, the Duke of Orleans, who became the regent of France and gladly appropriated absolute power. Under his reign the morals of the country were destined to sink to levels lower than ever before. No one in France led a more scandalous life than Philip. He was openly accused of practically every transgression imaginable—from murder to unnatural relations with his daughter. If the people of France could erase the seven years of his reign from the pages of history they no doubt would do so with relish and relief.

Though not a man of the exterme low morals of the Duke, Louis XIV had not been a saint either. Illegitimate children were only one of his specialties. He also believed in the adage that you can't take it with you. He spent everything he could lay his hands on and considerable amounts that he couldn't. When he died the country's coffers were $65 million in debt. Consequently, France was grappling for a means to survive financially when the Duke took over the mantle of leadership.

Along came a most unusual Scotsman named John Law. He favored, as Louis XIV had, spending at every opportunity. An extremely bright young man, Law was considered by some to be a borderline genius.

He was well-read and regarded as a mathematical whiz—an aptitude which led him to earn a living through gambling; he knew the odds well. When Lady Luck was not on his side he simply lived with and off of other men's wives. Besides a liberal quantity of ladies, Law liked good food and fine wines. He was a jetsetter of his time.

From the wives of bankers, with whom he had caroused, Law

had learned of a banking theory based on credit. Developing the principle further, he traveled across Europe trying to peddle this idea of a completely new financial system to any country that would listen. All turned thumbs down . . . all except the Duke of Orleans.

It must have been pre-ordained that Law and Philip would cross paths. In more ways than one they were two of a kind. The Duke and his country were in dire financial straits. His love of gambling and losses therefrom forced him to grab at straws. He agreed to try John Law's financial scheme.

Law's first move called for establishing a bank. This he did shortly after May 2, 1716, during the time of the planning of the small city which we now call New Orleans.

The Scot convinced investors they would reap royalties from companies that would spring forth and thrive in the city near the mouth of the great river. He painted a glowing picture to prospects: The city would control the economy of all of North America. It would be the cornucopia of the continent . . . the vessel at the bottom of the funnel. Products heading to world markets would have to exit through New Orleans where tariffs would have to be paid; products entering the continent would likewise have to come through that narrow door. Tariffs again!

John Law was a shrewd and adept traveling salesman. Not content merely with financial matters, he quickly became involved with other aspects in the founding of the new community, including the naming of the city and its streets. Appealing to French pride he saw to it that all names would have a French *raison d'etre*.

The new city, he proposed, should be called *La Nouvelle Orléans* after the Duke of Orleans. The Duke was in power and had been responsible for sustaining Law's biggest scheme to date. Streets would be named after France's ruling clique, in honor of a few favorite saints of the royal family and after investors in his new bank.

It was to be a royal city, so there would be a Royal Street. Law told the Duke of Orleans that the main street would be named "Orleans," and because of the Duke's importance, the street would be seven feet wider than any other. There would be a Chartres Street, as the Duke of Orleans had a son who held the title of Duke of Chartres. There had to be a Philip Street (which became St.

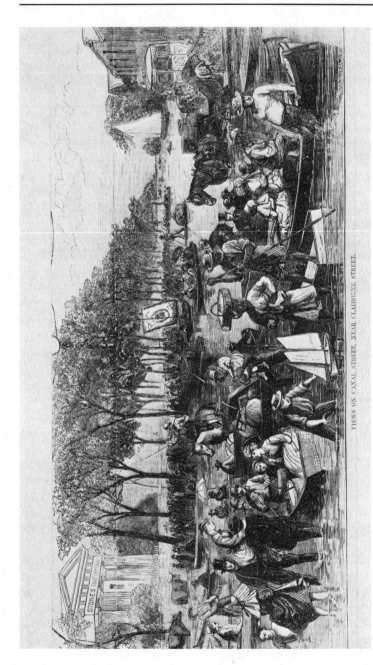

VIEWS ON CANAL STREET, NEAR CLAIBORNE STREET.

Although Canal Street has never been a canal, the break in the levee at Bonnet Carré in 1871 flooded New Orleans and turned the famed artery and other streets into "canals." (The Historic New Orleans Collection)

Philip), named after the patron saint of the House of Orleans. A
Bourbon Street had to be included because the Duke of Bourbon
was the largest investor in the bank and the Bourbons had more
money than any other family in France. The little king's father had
been the Duke of Burgundy so there should be a Burgundy Street.
Since the little king's Christian name was Louis, why not have one
named St. Louis Street?

Not all of the decisions were easy; a serious problem arose as
to how John Law would honor the names of two of Louis XIV's
illegitimate sons known as the "Royal Bastards," without anger-
ing the Duke of Orleans. Law confronted his engineer, Adrian
dePauger, with the dilemma, and it was decided the problem could
be solved in the following manner. The Duke of Orleans had to be
convinced that his personal feelings should not stand in the way
of this important undertaking. He was politely reminded that two
of the old King's twelve illegitimate children had reached high levels in government, were quite influential and their names would
have to be incorporated into the new city. They reemphasized to
the Duke that his street would be the main street in the center of
the new city and would be wider than any other. Orleans Street
would be flanked on each side by two Christian names, St. Peter
and St. Ann, followed by the "Royal Bastards," Toulouse and Du-
maine and again flanked by two Christians, St. Philip and St. Louis.
In other words, "his street," Orleans, would be buffered from the
"Royal Bastards" by saints.

The Duke of Orleans bought this scheme, and this was the
reasoning process from which the major street names in the French
Quarter evolved.

A number of these have changed over the years. The present
names are found on the bottom of street signs; the previous ap-
pellations are above.

CANAL STREET—NEUTRAL GROUND

To understand why Canal Street is such a wide street and how
the term "neutral ground" came to be, it is necessary to go back to
the time before the Louisiana Purchase of 1803. The City of New
Orleans had been successfully run by the Creoles of both France
and Spain since its inception in 1718. The only real contact the Cre-

oles had with Americans was with the rough and tumble men of the river. The Creoles had a favorite term for these Americans: they called them the "alligator men," indicating they had absolutely no fondness or respect for these barbaric beings. The less they had to deal with them the better.

With this negative impression it is easy to understand why the Creoles were so disturbed with the Louisiana Purchase. Most of their dealings with Americans up to that time had been with these "alligator men." As Americans moved into the city after the Purchase they were not welcomed by the Creoles, and therefore, moved upriver to start their own community.

Between the two areas a wide open space was left to separate the two factions; hence this strip became known as "neutral ground." If either the Americans or the Creoles crossed the strip into the other's territory, they literally took their lives into their own hands.

A serious problem arose for the Americans since they were not allowed to use the Carondelet Canal to get commerce and food in and out of the city. Until after the Civil War the mouth of the Mississippi River was closed because of sandbars for six or seven months of the year; and therefore, most products that entered the city from the Gulf entered it by going through Lake Borgne, Lake Pontchartrain to Bayou St. John and then through the Carondelet Canal, which ended at the edge of the French Quarter (area of Municipal Auditorium today). The end of the Carondelet Canal had a turning basin so that the ships could return to Lake Pontchartrain; hence the name Basin Street.

The Americans did not have the use of these facilities and went to the Congress of the United States for relief. On March 3, 1807, an Act of Congress was passed extending the Carondelet Canal down what is now Basin Street to what is now Canal Street and to the river, thereby fulfilling a local dream since the adolescence of New Orleans—the connection of the Mississippi River and Lake Pontchartrain.

The Canal was to be 50 feet wide and there would be a service road on each side 60½ feet wide, making the total width 171 feet.

One problem: Congress advanced $30,000 to an Irish contractor for the digging of the canal; he went to South America and

Canal Street, 171 feet wide, is the widest thoroughfare in the United States. (Louisiana Tourist Commission)

became a plantation owner. Never was a single spade of earth turned to dig the proposed waterway.

When you consider that Venice, Italy, with 28 miles of canals within the city, is known world-wide as the city of canals, it is ironic that New Orleans, with 87 miles of open canals, is seldom thought of in the same vein. Besides the 87 miles of canals there is the Mississippi River and 85 miles of canals below the surface of the streets that people never see. So we have a city of canals without recognition of that distinction, and a street named Canal without a canal on, under or near it.

Because of the animosities between the Americans and the Creoles, street names changed upon reaching Canal Street and heading upriver. As an example, Royal Street in the French Quarter became St. Charles at Canal.

The street named Canal is only three-and-a-half miles in length. It is born in the fertile womb of the Mother Mississippi and dies at the gates of a cemetery. Because it is our main street, New Orleans becomes the only major city in North America without a street named Main.

In 1854 when Judah Touro died, he left a sizable sum of money for the beautification of Canal Street in front of his store. Since it was such a handsome sum the City Council wanted to show its appreciation for what this man had done for the city, so they renamed Canal Street, Touro Avenue. But Canal Street was a street so beloved by the citizens of New Orleans that on May 19, 1855, the City Council met and quietly adopted an ordinance changing the name back to the original Canal Street. The people never stopped calling it Canal. Not one legal document during that one-year-plus period ever mentions the name of the street as Touro Avenue.

GALLATIN STREET—HELL ON EARTH

There are today two short blocks in the French Quarter called French Market Place. The location is directly behind the U.S. Mint and runs from Barracks to Ursuline Street. Nearby, truck farmers have fruit stands and a flea market is held on weekends. Before the area was known as French Market Place the two blocks were known as Gallatin Street.

Street signs in the French Quarter show both the present and former street names. (Noel Blakely)

In the nineteenth century these two blocks near the New Orleans riverfront were considered the roughest two blocks in the world. Some claimed they were more notorious than the entire Barbary Coast. It had taken a great deal of effort to gain the reputation as the most noted cesspool of immorality, flagrant wickedness and crime on the face of the earth. A writer, after visiting Gallatin Street gave the following description.

> It is likened to Sodom and Gomorrah of old. The harlots of Gallatin Street, and the proprietors who owned them, established new lows to which human beings might sink. Every known human vice was indulged in, with the exception of gambling; on Gallatin Street it was not necessary to gamble to get the clientele's money. When the prostitutes and the bars concluded their fleecing, if a man left Gallatin Street with any money in his pockets at all it was considered a miracle. Even the Police Force of the City of New Orleans refused to go into Gallatin Street 'day or night, no matter how many men were available; Gallatin Street had its own law, as bad as it was.

From dawn to dusk the street was deserted, as if its occupants were vampires who slept while the sun was out to be rested for the shadows of night.

No one in his right mind ever went to Gallatin Street alone day or night. Even parties in a group were putting their lives on the line. A wealthy young Creole named Parmalee made the mistake of going there with a group of friends while he was slightly intoxicated. He was never seen again. His prominent family did everything possible to find out what happened to him. Only by chance, a year later, did the family learn that the prostitute who had collared him in one of the dancing halls had hocked the ring she had stolen from him that night. And on her death bed she told the story of how he, along with a group of other young men, were shanghaied and sold to the captain of the sailing ship *Eberhard*. Newspaper accounts of the *Eberhard* indicate the ship sunk off the coast of Norway several months after leaving the Port of New Orleans. All hands were lost.

Life was held very cheaply under the dimly lit lamps of Gallatin Street. Muggings, murder, shanghais, the mutilation of bodies and other unimaginable horrors of life were a nightly occurrence. It was here that many of the ferocious animal fights, especially dog versus rat killings, were frequently held.

Dance halls on Gallatin Street were all laid out in similar fashion. The bar ran completely against the back wall of the building; six feet or so in front of the bar were planks on top of barrels where large, muscular, mean-looking bouncers sat ready at all times with the tools of their trade: clubs, knives, sling shots and brass knuckles on both hands. The bouncers allowed ordinary fights and even murders, provided the killers dragged out their victims. But they sprang immediately into action if property damage was threatened. They were also available to throw out those who had been drugged and robbed by the prostitutes on the second and third floors. The enforcers also had the authority to stop the music and clear the dance floor of couples who were engaged in activities other than dancing. It was not uncommon for all those inside the dance hall to be completely nude in a *ménage à* many.

One of the popular places on Gallatin Street was the "Green Tree," a three-story establishment opened in 1850 by an old woman named Morgan. Indeed, she must have been a tough cookie, for she was one of the few to survive ownership. She sold it to Harry Rice before any major incident happened to her. Harry unfortunately made some sailors angry by unduly watering their liquor, and in return they stoned him to the brink of death.

The next owner was Mary Rice, better known to her intimate friends as "one-legged Duffy," who was dragged into the shed behind the dance hall, stabbed five times, and for good measure, beaten unmercifully over the head with her own wooden leg until she died.

Then came Paddy Welsh, a tough Irishman who thought he was tougher than the gang of ruffians, called The Live Oak Boys, who ran Gallatin Street at will. He told them without hesitation to stay out of his establishment. They came anyway, wrecked the place and told him not to open again. He ignored the warning and reopened. On the next day he disappeared and two days later his body, with the skull crushed, was found floating in the river.

Enter William Lee, an ex-drum major of the United States Army. Over a simple disagreement he was killed by Bill Knuckly, a member of The Live Oak Boys.

The last owner, Tom Pickett, was a real tough dude who ran the business with an iron fist and made a good profit in the process. The Live Oak Boys once again raided the place, causing considerable damage. Pickett knew who did it and decided to take justice into his own hands. Fortifying himself with enough liquor to give him sufficient courage to even up the score, he started out in search of the members of the Live Oak gang with pistols in both hands. Finding them in a saloon on Levee Street, he walked behind Jack Lowe, one of the members, and without batting an eye, shot him through the head. He turned and fired at Bill Knuckly, but Bill's brother, Mike, jumped between the two and was shot through the heart and killed instantly. Pickett was brought to trial and sentenced to life imprisonment.

That is what happened to the owners of only one of the many establishments on Gallatin Street. If their lives were that violent, imagine what happened to the every day employees and patrons in these establishments.

It is interesting to note that many of the businesses were owned and operated by females, and they were some of the toughest people on Gallatin Street.

One of the bars was quite unique. The back wall of the bar was designed like the walled "ovens" in the cemetery. A sign on top read appropriately, "Rest in Peace." Bartenders were all dressed as undertakers and the liquors—Scotch, Bourbon, Gin and Rum—were secured in small coffins that were pulled from the ovens when a drink was ordered. This "trough" had a reputation for cutting its drinks with creosote to give it more kick.

It is ironic that Gallatin Street was named for a very righteous man named Albert Gallatin. Secretary of the Treasury of the United States in President Thomas Jefferson's cabinet, he apparently was a beloved man throughout the country. Counties in Kentucky and Montana are named in his honor. Cities in Missouri, Illinois and Tennessee, as well as a river, a national forest, and a mountain pass in the northwest carry his name. New Orleans believed it was honoring him by naming a street in his honor, but it became one of the hell holes of this earth . . . the toughest two blocks anywhere.

THE CITY'S FIRST CIRCLE AND AVENUE

Shortly after New Orleans was founded in 1718, the area where New Orleans' first circle and avenue were later to be built became the property of the governor of Louisiana, Bienville. A land grant from a grateful government to a very capable explorer, this property was a favorite hunting place for Governor Bienville, as it was close to his fishing camp located on a small lake at the present-day intersection of Baronne and Poydras Streets.

The Bienville property was also the first land in New Orleans to be sold. Governor Bienville sold the 84 arpents of frontage on the river, (which ran from present-day Bienville Street to approximately Felicity Street and from the river to approximately Claiborne Avenue), to the religious Order of the Jesuits for a plantation. On it the Jesuits introduced oranges and sugarcane to North America. Unfortunately, the Jesuits encountered political/governmental hostility and were banished from Louisiana. Their land was sold at public auction to four separate owners: Delord Sarpy, Thomas Soulet, Jacques Livaudais and Robin Delogny.

In 1806 the City of New Orleans, on the American side, was ready for expansion as more and more Americans were arriving after the Louisiana Purchase of 1803. Barthelemy Lafon was a man of vision and one who literally had his finger in every economic pie in the city. He was the city's surveyor, map maker, a large property owner, printer, architect, engineer, theater manager and also a pirate (he dealt in smuggled contraband). Lafon was also a promoter. The land running from where St. Charles Street ended, going upriver, was viewed by him as well-suited for creation of a city of the future. His first objective was to design a continuation of that street in a large curve because if it continued in the direction it was going it would run directly into the river. Therefore, he conceived a circle whereby he could turn the street so that it would parallel the river.

He further hoped that this, the city's first circle, would serve as a meeting place for Americans to compete with the Creoles' *Place d'Arms* (Jackson Square). In designing the circle, he planned to install a Tivoli (merry-go-round) in the center, therefore, he decided to name it Tivoli Circle. A graceful waterway, spanned by foot bridges, would ring the circle.

Lafon also felt that in order to attract attention to his new city he would make the street going upriver from Tivoli Place into the city's first avenue—a broad passageway bordered by trees. Up until this time all New Orleans streets were simple and narrow. The new avenue would hopefully attract attention.

This era, the early 1800s, is known as the era of "Greek Revival" throughout the United States. Some of the cities born during that period were Athens, Georgia; Troy and Ithaca, New York; and eleven cities named after Sparta. Our nation's capital, Washington, D.C., was built in the early 1800s during the Greek Revival Era in the United States.

If that was the style people liked at the time, Lafon would give it to them. The street leading to the circle from the lake would be called Triton Walk. Triton, son of Greek gods Neptune and Amphitrite, was half-man and half-fish.

From the circle to the river the street would have a different name. It was named Delord Street after Delord Sarpy, one of the previous plantation owners. Lafon did not want to be accused of favoritism: he named St. Thomas Street after Thomas Soulet, St. James for Jacques Livaudais, and Celeste for Jacques' wife. Since Jacques Livaudais' plantation was named Annunciation, he named one of the streets Annunciation Street. For Robin Delogny, he named Robin Street (no longer in existence, but there is still a wharf on the riverfront named Robin Wharf), and Constance Street after Delogny's wife. Two smaller land owners in the new city were Messrs. Poeyfarre and Gaiennie. He also named streets after them as a courtesy.

One of the previous plantation owners sported his very own race course, so he named one of the streets Race Street. Since the Jesuits once had an orange grove on this land, he designated an Orange Street. Because there was a religious order of nuns in this area, he named Religious Street, Nuns Street, and Felicity Street after the assistant Mother Superior, Sister Saint Felicity. Unfortunately, a careless map maker left out the word "Saint" and the error was never corrected. Until this date the name remains simply Felicity.

Every neighborhood in old New Orleans had its market, so there was to be a Market Street. And since every city in Greece had a Prytaneum dedicated to Hestia, goddess of the hearth, he would name one of the streets Prytania.

Next came the important task of finding a name for the city's first avenue, and he named it Naydes (later changed to St. Charles Avenue). In Greek mythology Naydes was a water nymph, and the street was so called because it was near the river. The streets heading toward the lake were called Apollo (god of the universe), Bacchus (god of wine), Dryades (wood nymphs—this street ran near the woods) and Hercules (god of strength).

Apollo is now Carondelet, Bacchus is now Baronne and Hercules is now Rampart. Although we still have a Dryades Street, we still mispronounce it by calling it Dri-ads.

Last of the streets to be named in the new city were the cross streets, heading from the circle going upriver, and once again Greek mythology was to play a leading role. These nine streets were named for the Greek muses, Calliope—"Epics," Clio—"History," Erato—"Lyrics," Thalia—"Comedy," Melpomene—"Tragedy," Terpsechore—"Dance," Euterpe—"Music," Polyhymnia— "Hymns" and Urania—"Astronomy."

Ingenious Barthelemy Lafon utilized every "avenue" available to fully promote his city of the future. It worked! In the mid-1980s the avenue he created is still one of the most beautiful in America. And the history of the area he designed will live forever.

In 1884 a statue of Robert E. Lee was erected, and the name of the circle was changed from Tivoli Circle to Lee Circle. The city on more than one occasion tried to change the name from Tivoli Circle to Tivoli Place and from Lee Circle to Lee Place, but each time the citizens rebelled, and "circle" it has been to this day. The statue of General Lee is facing North. An old joke maintains that the YMCA across the street was built to remind Lee that the Yankees Might Come Again!

Anti-lottery cartoon. (The Historic New Orleans Collection)

CHAPTER FOUR

*C*rime-Gambling

 In its formative years New Orleans was inhabited to a considerable extent by an element of practicing criminals. When Bienville came over to establish the city he recruited a handful of professionals: lawyers, doctors and engineers. He also brought along a much larger group to do the physical work in clearing the land. This contingent included some 80 of the lowest criminal element to be found in the jails of France.

In 1719 a ship arrived at the Port of New Orleans with 189 passengers, some 106 of whom were not exactly law-abiding innocents. There were: seven tobacco smugglers, three dealers in contraband salt, ten vagabonds from Lyon and six from Orléans, 20 women who had been caught engaging in fraud and 60 women from the Rockfort House of Correction—a "class act" if ever there was one!

Ship after ship came with holds filled with the seamy side of low-lifers. Why was the recruiting campaign for "warm bodies" producing such a menagerie of wickedness? Remember John Law? It was his doing. The Scotsman was using leverage again.

His contract with authorities called for a set number of Frenchmen to be in New Orleans at appointed times. Perhaps it was because it was hard for Frenchmen to separate from the mother land . . . or maybe the hazards of an ocean voyage in those days

were too formidable. Law circulated posters advertising New Orleans as a land of milk and honey with abundant food and beautiful women. But word from the early arrivals confirmed that all
they found were alligators, mosquitos and snakes. Whatever the
reasons, Law was having trouble meeting his quotas to fulfill his
contract. Apparently his pledge did not specify the *kinds* of people
he would attract to New Orleans. So he employed the help of new
laws which had been enacted at his urging, to satisfy the letter of
his agreement. The first statute stipulated that anyone out of work
for four consecutive days could suffer the penalty of being shipped
to Louisiana. Prostitutes engaged in an illegal profession were
technically out of work and could be sent to *La Nouvelle Orléans* with
dispatch.

The second law gave total freedom to any man in a French
jail, regardless of his crime, provided he marry a prostitute and
agree to go to Louisiana. It is far-fetched to imagine a convict who
would elect to rot in jail rather than take an all expense paid voyage to distant lands with a traveling companion of considerable experience. Ships transporting the hordes of honeymooners were apt
forerunners of modern-day "love boats." But a connubial cruise
does not a felon reform, so when the malefactors arrived in New
Orleans they continued their wayward habits. Crime was nothing
short of rampant!

The first recorded crime in New Orleans took place in 1720,
shortly after the city was founded. Jean Baptiste Portier was found
guilty of stealing a towel from a home where he was staying. For
his sentence he was flogged every hour by slaves for three consecutive days, his personal belongings were sold and all proceeds
were taken by the government. To top it off he was sentenced to
three years at hard labor and branded as a thief. He would carry
the title of criminal for life. The crime was something minor but the
punishment, although regarded today as rather harsh, was typical
for the times. Punishment for a major offense was horrifying, to
wit:

In 1754 three mutineer refugees killed Ducrox, a harsh French
commandant at Camp Island near Fort Biloxi. They were found
guilty and paid dearly.

Two of the men were strapped, spread eagle, to wagon
wheels and rolled into *Place d'Arms*. Each was left lashed to the

Public hangings, common until 1880, were usually held in Jackson Square. (Drawing by Calvin Balencie)

wheel in the sun for a full day. On the following morning their bones were broken one by one by slaves wielding massive sledge hammers. The third mutineer was not quite as lucky. He was nailed alive to the inside of a wooden coffin and the coffin was then sawed in half.

In 1771 Luis de Unzaga, Governor of Louisiana, condemned two Negro slaves, Mirliton and Temba, to death by strangulation for murdering their master. They were brought out of the prison, haltered around the neck and hands and dragged through the streets from the tail of a pack horse. The town crier preceded the agonizing procession, announcing the crime that the slaves had committed. Through the streets of the French Quarter they were dragged on their journey to the gallows where they were hanged until dead. After the execution Temba's hands and feet were cut off. The ears of both Mirliton and Temba were cut off close to their heads. Hands, feet and/or ears were often required by law to be nailed on posts at the entrance gates to the city and left there until consumed by animals or elements. The penalty for removing the bone-chilling exhibits was death. Left hanging in Jackson Square, the bodies of Mirliton and Temba were to serve as a deterrent to others who might consider taking the law into their own hands.

Pedro and Carlos were two minor accomplices in the Temba-Mirliton affair. Carlos was tarred and feathered and exposed in the streets for several days on the back of a pack animal. Pedro, the hapless accessory, was given 100 lashes at the foot of the gallows where Temba and Mirliton were hung.

Almost all punishment in the early days of New Orleans was administered in *Place d'Arms* (Jackson Square) so that all citizens could attend, thereby serving as a restraint to further crime.

Up until the turn of the century those who were sentenced to jail faced serious survival problems. Until the 1880s records indicate that the mortality rate for prisoners was somewhere between 50 and 80 percent. Prior to 1898 anyone receiving a sentence for more than 10 years was not expected to come out alive. Before 1898 all penal institutions were leased to private enterprises, operators of which were anxious to produce a product, sell it and make a profit. Overhead was held to a minimum by working inmates as much as humanly possible seven days a week and feeding them only enough to keep them alive.

While laws were not to be taken lightly, there were a great many to be observed and some were utterly ridiculous. For example, it was actually against the law during the French and Spanish control of Louisiana to commit suicide.

Under both French and Spanish possession (both being Catholic nations), it was against the law in Louisiana to follow any religion other than Catholic. Since it was against the laws of the Church to commit suicide it was also against the laws of the State. The body of anyone who had the audacity to take his or her life was brought to court, found guilty and given the standard sentence. It was dragged through the streets of the French Quarter (for the convenience of senior citizens who might not get to see the body in the square). The body was then hung in the square until the stench was unbearable. But the worst possible fate for the Christian was yet to come. The suicide victim was denied burial in consecrated ground and the body was thrown into the swamp for animals to ravage. No civil rights for criminals here.

NEW ORLEANS' FIRST ATTEMPT AT LEGALIZED GAMBLING

In 1763 Governor Jean Jacques Blaise Dabbadie, in an official report to France, complained bitterly that the people of New Orleans were wholly given to gambling. They gambled on the contents of the King's warehouse, the numbers on currency, in fact, he said, they would gamble on anything and everything.

Laws were instituted against wagering, but to no avail. Heavy fines were levied along with 25 lashes on the bare back. But before the scars on the backs had healed the odds-takers were back again at their favorite games of chance.

After much debate it was decided that since people insisted on gambling, it would be better to have a few houses filled with gamesters than to have hundreds of them scattered across the city with the attendant rabble-rousing. Placing this vice under banner of law and order would not only afford better control, it would be a good source of funds for Charity Hospital and other benevolent purposes. Summing up their feelings, "we should compel the devil to pay tribute to virtue," city fathers in 1823 finally made Lady Luck

The illustration shows Confederate Generals Beauregard and Early and their aides drawing for prizes. Charity Hospital, top center, was the beneficiary of $40,000 annually from the Louisiana Lottery. (The Historic New Orleans Collection)

an honest woman, as gambling was finally legalized in New Orleans and Louisiana.

Six "gambling temples," as they were called, were opened and each contributed $5,000 annually toward the support of Charity Hospital and the College of Orleans. The immoral aspects of the legislation were opposed by men of the cloth, including Timothy Flint, a New England clergyman, who charged that the city was disgraced by licensed gambling. With growing pressure the "temple" doors were finally sealed in 1836, bringing to an end New Orleans' first attempt at legalized gambling.

But from 1823 to 1836, a period of 13 years, gambling in New Orleans and Louisiana was legal, controlled and did show a profit. Apparently 13 was an unlucky number for it, too.

Illegal or not, it would be safe to wager that there is as much gambling going on in New Orleans today as there ever was when gambling was legal.

THE LOUISIANA LOTTERY

Gambling in New Orleans enjoyed a resurgence and reached its zenith during the days of carpetbag rule. Virtually a gambling haven by the end of that era, the city had 83 large gambling establishments in full operation.

In 1868 the carpetbag legislature presented Charles T. Howard and his six associates with a state lottery charter. The Louisiana Lottery agreed to pay $40,000 per year to New Orleans Charity Hospital in return for this exclusive 25-year franchise.

Believe it or not the monopolistic Louisiana Lottery showed no profit in the first two years of operation. Then one of the employees, an Irishman named Maximilian A. Dauphin, came forth with a bold proposal. A physician in his homeland, the good doctor had been forced to leave the Emerald Isle because of his political beliefs. A bookkeeper for the Louisiana Lottery for a short time, he sought to convince Howard and his associates that they had a golden goose but were unable to make it lay because of their lack of knowledge. Just as he could make an incision into the human body to make the necessary repairs that would allow it to function properly, he proposed an incision into the pockets of potential lottery customers and maintained he had the ability to do it successfully. For his services he demanded a salary of $50,000 a year. Howard and his associates asked him what he planned to do. Politely he told them he was not stupid, knowing he would not receive a dime if he revealed his plan. Under their noses he continued to dangle the possibility of making vast sums of money, and it worked; once again greed prevailed.

They were convinced by the good physician and he came through with his promises. Quickly he identified the problem as lack of trust: people simply did not believe the game was fair. To convince them that it *was* he proceeded to hire two ex-Confederate Generals, P. G. T. Beauregard and Jubal A. Early. Cost $30,000. Their jobs: to draw the lottery numbers. Their prestige and reputations instilled confidence and trust, and the number of customers spiralled. Price of stock in the Louisiana Lottery rose rapidly from $35.00 to $1,200 per share.

Thus the gambling venture that almost went broke was saved through the "pocket surgery" of a physician named Maximilian A. Dauphin from good old Ireland.

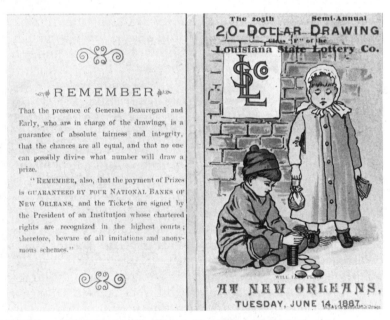

Pro-lottery advertisement. (The Historic New Orleans Collection)

By 1890 a flood of money was coming in as the jackpots continued to grow in value. In that year the lottery took in $30 million tax-free. During that same year, a local barber with a $20 ticket scalped the Louisiana Lottery for $300,000. And that was in the days when a shave and a haircut were less than 15¢.

In September, 1890, the U.S. Congress enacted a law prohibiting the use of the mails for the transmission of all letters, circulars and newspapers relating to the business of lottery. Two years later the Louisiana Lottery died when Governor Francis T. Nicholls refused to sign the renewal of the charter of the Louisiana Lottery Company. The appetite of Orleanians to gamble would be satiated elsewhere.

CRAPS

Bernard Mandeville deMarigny was the son of Pierre deMarigny, and at the time, New Orleans' and Louisiana's wealthiest businessman. Pierre had rubbed elbows with numerous other great men in his lifetime. When the Duc d'Orléans, Louis Philippe, the future Regent of France, visited New Orleans in 1798, he was entertained at the home of Pierre deMarigny. After dining lavishly they retired to the parlor, lit their Havana Cigars with $100 bills and thought nothing of it.

When Pierre died in 1803, Bernard, now 18 years of age and full of vim and vigor, was heir to his father's millions, not to mention the vast land holdings below New Orleans (now Faubourg Marigny). Bernard's uncle and guardian, Ignace de Lino de Chalmette, could do nothing to control Bernard. He decided to get him out from under his feet by sending Bernard to Europe to be educated. Bernard was a strong-headed invididual who did what he wanted. After all, he was a millionaire with more than enough money to insure his independence.

Unfortunately, when Bernard returned to New Orleans he appeared to have learned only one thing in his training in Europe. He had become addicted to a game called "Chance." It was named Chance because the player took a big chance whenever he played this volatile game. It consisted of two small square white cubes with either one, two, three, four, five, or six black dots on each side. When the cubes were thrown on a surface the total combined dots showing on the top of the cubes determined a win or a loss.

Keel boatmen from Kentucky, Tennessee, Ohio and other states up and down the river came to New Orleans and sought out Bernard to play Chance. Not only was he loaded with money, he wasn't very good at the game he loved so much.

Like most Frenchmen, Bernard loved to eat frog legs. As he enjoyed his favorite diversion he nibbled on the fried delicacies. Corrupting the French word for frog, *crapaud*, the rivermen began saying they couldn't wait to get to New Orleans to play Chance with Johnny "Craps." Hence the game of "Chance" evolved into the game of "Craps."

Bernard Mandeville deMarigny, the last of the truly great Creole gentlemen, died in 1868 at age 83. He saw his beloved city fly under French, Spanish, Confederate and American flags. He also saw some of his millions fly away on the game he introduced to North America. It is safe to say there will never be another like him because the conditions that produced this character have long disappeared. But he will be remembered for two things: He was the first millionaire playboy on the North American continent and he was responsible for the game called "Craps." A legacy of sorts, if you like.

CHAPTER FIVE

*D*rainage and Canals

 Although the Choctaw Indians trekked back and forth over the land presently known as New Orleans, they probably never entertained any notion of living permanently in this marshy bog. Not only was the area bottomless swampland, but the river also flooded it at frequent intervals. Heavy rainfall inundated the terrain as a matter of course, and the Choctaws had never learned to swim.

The savages probably guffawed to the point of suffocation watching the white man laying out the town in ankle-deep, if not hip-deep water. By then the Indians had probably learned that you can always tell a Frenchman . . . but you can't tell him much.

The annual New Orleans rainfall of 58.16 inches amounts to 12½ billion cubic feet weighing 390 million tons. No other U.S. city with a population over 500,000 receives as much annual precipitation and there is little in the way of natural drainage. In New Orleans there is virtually no "downhill."

Our city can be likened to a bowl. Because it is below sea level, flood protection from the river and lake comes from man-made levees. When approximately five feet of rain falls annually into the bowl it must be removed mechanically. Even though drainage has been its principal problem since the city was founded in 1718, an overall comprehensive plan took a long time aborning.

The city's first drainage system consisted of simple man-made canals which relied on gravity to drain the city into surrounding swamps. Unfortunately, after heavy rains water levels in the swamps rose quickly and frequently flowed back into the city. Like an overflowing commode, the resulting sights and smells were repulsive. To keep from walking in the mire, mud was piled up and wooden boards were laid atop the dry "gumbo." Walkways looked like church benches, hence the term *banquette* (a low bench) was used to denote the walks. In New Orleans sidewalks are still called "banquettes."

After the Louisiana Purchase in 1803 the high and dry land was soon occupied completely. Consequently, by 1830 a "wishy-washy" attempt was made to drain some of the wet land to make it more habitable. It was not a well thought-out plan. By 1890 the only real improvement was the installation of four 30-foot (in diameter) wooden, engine-driven water wheels with a capacity of 545,000 gallons per minute. The pumps were located on Dublin Street near Carrollton Avenue, Melpomene and South Claiborne streets, Bienville and Hagen Avenue (now Jefferson Davis Avenue), and London Avenue and Gentilly.

It became obvious to leading citizens in 1893 that a master plan to keep the city dry would have to be devised if the metropolis was to grow. In that same year the city's first topographical survey was made. During the next decade the following progress ensued:

In 1895 a master plan for drainage was presented;

In 1896 the New Orleans Drainage Commission was organized;

Construction of the present drainage system was started in 1897;

In 1899 the Sewerage and Water Board was authorized;

In 1903 New Orleans' Drainage Commission and Sewerage and Water Board merged.

Today, the drainage system of the Crescent City encompasses 87 miles of large, open-drainage canals plus 85 miles of closed canals, some measuring up to 97 feet across. (These could accommodate up to ten cars abreast.) The closed canals are by far the most efficient of the two, providing greater capacity and more uniform velocity than the open variety. Exorbitant costs would be involved in converting to closed canals and probably preclude conversion in

Prior to the use of highly efficient, mechanical drainage pumps built by Albert Baldwin Woods, New Orleans leaders attempted to drain the city by use of four 30-foot-diameter wooden water wheels like this one that was located at Dublin and Oleander streets. (Photo furnished by the New Orleans Sewerage and Water Board)

the forseeable future. Replacement value of the drainage system is estimated at two-and-a-half billion dollars. Thank Providence it is in place . . . especially when the gully washers come.

Besides the primary canals New Orleans also has 227 miles of primary pipe-collecting systems which are tied in with 1,258 miles of sub-surface drainage pipe. If all of the Sewerage and Water Board drain pipes were laid end to end, they would extend from New Orleans to Seattle, Washington.

The topographical survey of 1893 demonstrated that rainwater pumped out of the city could best be handled by pumping it into Lake Pontchartrain and Bayou Bienville. Today, the Intracoastal Waterway and the Mississippi River-Gulf Outlets are also used as crucibles. It is not feasible to lift such immense quantities of water over the levees and into the Mississippi River.

The heaviest rainfall ever recorded in New Orleans' history was 14.94 inches in only 19 hours. It was on Good Friday, April 15, 1927. The heaviest rain over a two-week period followed the massive hurricane of 1915 when New Orleans recorded 22 inches of rain in two weeks.

The city today has 20 drainage pumping stations with a total of 89 pumps with a capacity of 15,642,000 gallons per minute of 22½ billion gallons per day. The combined capacity of the 89 pumps could stop the flow of the Ohio River. And the enormous capacity of the pumping system could completely empty a 10 square mile lake 10 feet deep in just 24 hours. That's a lot of suction!

Even if New Orleans were to have an unusual dry spell lasting as long as 90 days some of the pumps would still have to be operated daily because of severe seepage from the river, the lake and the swamps surrounding the city.

Over 300 billion gallons of Mississippi River water flow by New Orleans daily which is twice the volume used by all 50 states each day.

The drainage pump with the largest capacity in the world is located on the 17th Street Canal between Metairie Road and Interstate 10. A total of 22 pumps, all 14 feet in diameter, are reported to be the largest in the world. Designed to be cleaned while in operation, they are equipped with dry chambers which allow access for maintenance workers to change bearings and to make minor repairs without interrupting service.

The largest drainage pumps in the world are 14 feet in diameter. New Orleans has 22 of them plus numerous smaller units. (Photo furnished by the New Orleans Sewerage and Water Board)

CITY'S WORST FLOOD

New Orleans' worst flood year in recorded history was 1927. It was not only a bad flood year for our city, but because of record flooding all along the Mississippi River and its tributaries the 1927 floods were the greatest national disaster in the history of the United States. Approximately 500,000 people were displaced and damage nationwide was estimated in the hundreds of millions of dollars.

During this national calamity, 14.94 inches of rain fell in New Orleans in only 19 hours. Levees had to be sandbagged to insure an additional three feet of protection, but even then water kept spilling over the top.

The sole source of electricity to the Sewerage and Water Board at the time was New Orleans Public Service, Inc., which lost all power on that fateful day. No power; no pumping. The city was inundated.

Because of the national and local disaster two vital ensuing programs have prevented another city-wide flood since 1927. The United States Corps of Engineers finally decided that levees were not sufficient to hold back the surges of the river at high stages. Therefore, pressure on the huge dikes was relieved by instituting four spillways: Bonnet Carré, Morganza, Atchafalaya, and Bohemia. All four have been used periodically and have served well the purpose for which they were built. Secondly, the Sewerage and Water Board, not wishing to be without electricity in an emergency again, built its own electric generating stations.

Since 1927 New Orleans has endured spot flooding from time to time. Hurricanes have driven walls of water up the ship channels, causing severe flooding. Unexpected high winds coming out of the north have pushed large quantities of water from Lake Pontchartrain into the Industrial Canal and through open flood gates. Heavy rainfalls in short periods of time have exceeded the capacity of drainage pumps. Drainage canals have been obstructed by washing machines, garbage cans, mattresses, old automobile tires, even old automobiles. These problems notwithstanding, the New Orleans Sewerage and Water Board drainage system is without a doubt one of the finest and most efficiently-operated in the world. The Board can and does take care of the average situation and makes the best of unusual circumstances.

It is probably as financially unfeasible and impractical to build a drainage system that would ward off any eventuality as it would be to air-condition a home to accommodate a rehearsal party of 30 guests on the evening before your daughter's wedding. True, it is difficult to accept that kind of reasoning when standing in water up to the armpits, but when you live in a city that is for the most part below sea level, flooding is always a threat, and residents of low-lying areas should be prepared.

Better to light one candle than to curse the Sewerage and Water Board.

RAIN

While our city is bathed with over 58 inches of precipitation annually it actually receives far less than that amount in rain. Snow? Perhaps an inch every dozen or more years. What then? Because of its geographic location the city receives (especially during the months of June, July and August) daily afternoon *thundershowers*, not rain. Although it is as wet as rain it would be safe to say 50 percent of the moisture that falls on our metro area is in the form of thundershowers.

Whether it be rain or thundershowers, it has always been blessed by some and cursed by others. Before the advent of gas and electric clothes dryers housewives cursed the rains on washday. The Summer Pops Concerts damned the rain on weekends. Before the days of air conditioning concerts were held outdoors; rain meant cancellation thereof and loss of money. During the week retail merchants blasphemed the downpours because they cut into their sales. Rain was cursed during the entire week by one group or another.

Conversely, rain has been a true blessing for our people, whether they appreciate it or not. Before the advent of sanitary drainage human waste lingered in the gutters in front of houses and businesses until the rain flushed it away. Those who had to tote water for drinking, bathing and cooking when wooden cisterns ran dry smiled at thundershowers. Before there were sheds to cover cargo on the river front, manufacturers of tarpaulins prayed for heavy rains. Children used the rain-filled streets and gutters as playgrounds and swimming pools.

With the high cost of utilities today the citizenry is blessed with the cooling effects of afternoon thundershowers. Because of a drought in the summer of 1981 residential electric bills soared to nearly 25 percent higher than in 1980, which had the usual rainy season. The vibrant, verdant gardens in patios, courtyards and backyards around the city will attest to the life-giving qualities of the moisture from the heavens. Plants appear to revel and rejoice at the first sound of thunder. It is said that it is not wise to stand too long in a Crescent City garden or a vine will grow up your leg.

In the mid-1800s Canal Street was the sight of a most unusual happening during a prolonged heavy rain. A soaked funeral procession was in progress heading from the river toward the lake while rain came down "in buckets." Because of the horrible weather conditions only the immediate family and a few intensely loyal friends chose to walk ahead of the horse-drawn funeral hearse. As the wagon rattled over the cobblestones at the intersection of Canal and Royal streets the coffin bounced out of the rear of the funeral hearse, floated to the gutter and began its way toward the river as the funeral proceeded toward its destination. A straggler yelled for assistance and rescued the body from a premature watery grave.

With increasing interest in television more than a few viewers consider it a waste to spend so much time discussing the weather on the tube. For the three summer months one show could be taped and shown daily for 90 days. There is little change from one day to the next: "The weather today will be hot and humid with the chance of afternoon thundershowers. Temperatures will get up to 98 degrees with 85 percent humidity."

After giving a talk on meteorology, one of the city's TV weathermen, Al Duckworth of Channel 4, was fielding a great deal of audience flak about accuracy, or the lack of it, in predicting the weather. With aplomb and diplomacy he responded, "Meteorology is truly a great profession. Who among you can be wrong in your work 50 percent of the time and not be fired?"

Duckworth was being modest. In New Orleans, the percentage of accuracy in predicting the weather is considerably higher . . . because weather patterns are considerably predictable.

For the first 125 to 150 years of New Orleans' existence canals played a vital roll not only in the conveyance of drainage water but as an economical means of moving the city's commerce.

During the Spanish regime Governor Carondelet extended the route on Bayou St. John with a canal he named in his honor. It ran from the end of Bayou St. John down present-day Orleans Avenue to what is now called Basin Street. This street takes its name from the turning basin existing at the end of the Carondelet Canal where sailing ships would turn to return to the lake. The Carondelet extension made it possible for the Spanish Creoles to receive supplies at points nearer their residences and businesses. Since roads were primitive and few in number, this was an extremely important capital improvement.

Representatives of the American sector had been successful in getting Congress to authorize an extension from the turning basin of the Carondelet Canal down present-day Basin Street to present-day Canal Street and then to the River. This would have tied the River and the Lake together, giving both the Creoles and the Americans access to an important waterway. Unfortunately, the Irish contractor absconded with the budget so the Americans decided to dig a canal of their own.

In 1832 an improvement bank was organized to handle the project. A viable and active institution and the first of its kind organized to finance a specific project, the Canal Bank served the city for many years.

Estimated cost of the New Basin Canal was approximately one-quarter of a million dollars; it eventually cost five times that amount. The New Basin Canal ran from Lake Pontchartrain down what is now the Pontchartrain Expressway to South Rampart Street.

Since the digging through swampland was extremely dangerous and because it was considered prohibitive to use "expensive" slaves as laborers, Irish immigrants were recruited. By the thousands they were brought to New Orleans to work at a salary of less than a dollar a day. The work did prove to be extremely hazardous; water seepage into the Canal required around-the-clock, hand-operation of wooden pumps like those designed by Archimedes in 287 B.C. Even with precaution, mud slides became frequent occurrences, literally burying men alive in the trench that would become the New Basin Canal.

The perils of working through swampland included frequent epidemics of cholera and yellow fever which ravaged the work force. Before the project was completed an estimated 8,000 Irish immigrants paid with their lives. Some were buried accidentally in the canal, others were buried on the banks within a few feet of where they had been killed. These were truly oppressive times for the Irish immigrants who were treated like beasts of burden. It is said that when an Irish worker died or was killed before noon his family would get only a half day's pay, if anything at all.

The canal was, nonetheless, completed in spite of the utmost in difficult terrain. When it was opened in just six short years the feat was cited as an engineering marvel rivaling the construction of the Panama Canal.

The Canal Bank Corporation was so successful, other improvement banks were set up to build gas works, water works, the St. Charles and St. Louis Hotels and numerous railroads.

The New Basin Canal was a phenomenal success. Collection of tolls for everything conveyed thereon reached one-and-a-half million dollars annually. Although the waterway more than served its purpose, progress would eventually render it obsolete. By constitutional amendment in 1946 the city of New Orleans authorized the filling of the canal which had taken six years to build. It had operated for 108 years. The channel ended up costing much more to fill than it had cost to build.

Those of us old enough to remember the New Basin Canal remember it with fond memories. As boys, my friends and I would ride and sway on the West End Boulevard streetcar which paralleled the waterway. Boarding the streetcar with hamper basket, crab nets and bait, a bottle of water and sandwiches, we would head for a day on the lake. As we rode along we saw the oyster luggers, fruit boats, vegetable boats and vessels transporting building materials and coal, going by slowly like a Mardi Gras parade inching toward the city. At our destination we would set out our nets, crab for a little while and amble on back towards town past the locks. After lunch we would conspire to aggravate the hired hands on one of the watermelon boats to the point that they would throw one of their juicy ones at us. We had watermelon for dessert more times than not.

I shall always remember those days and the canal built with the muscle and upon the bones of the hungry and homeless Irish.

No wonder their survivors are such a cohesive ethnic group in our city. In a legacy of hardship, friendship and loyalty run deep.

The Legacy of Albert Baldwin Wood

Disposing of some five feet of rain annually, not to mention the perpetual seepage from the river, the lake and the swamps, was at one time believed to be of such enormous proportions as to be unachievable. Yet 320 million tons of water *are* removed from the city of New Orleans annually and this is accomplished with more efficiency than anywhere else. Although legions of dedicated people were immersed in meeting this challenge, the single individual who contributed the most was Albert Baldwin Wood. A member of the Sewerage and Water Board from its inception, a native Orleanian, graduate of Tulane University, an electrical engineer—he was responsible for designing and building the A. B. Wood screw pumps. These not only had the phenomenal capacity to rid the cityscape of its exceptionally high volume of rain but they were also designed to continue operating in spite of the usual obstructions.

The A. B. Wood screw pumps were so efficient and dependable that they have been used throughout the world where similar conditions prevail, including the Zeider Zee in Holland.

Wood holds the distinction of having designed and built the largest drainage pump ever. Without its impeller, the fourteen-foot in diameter, water-sucking monster is large enough to accommodate a two-and-a-half ton truck.

Another solution manifesting ingenuity and engineering know-how was the handling of the water from the Broad Street canal to Bayou Bienvenu. The Broad Street pumping station and Bayou Bienvenu are separated by the 26-foot-deep Industrial Canal which is large enough to handle ocean-going vessels. Pumped from the Broad Street pumping station the water travels 26 feet below the Industrial Canal by means of the world's largest siphon. When the water reaches the other side of the canal pumps send it to Bayou Bienvenu.

Holding numerous patents during his lifetime, Wood was considered around the world as the leader in his field. Although he helped solve the drainage problems of many cities abroad, he seldom traveled out of his treasured city, preferring instead to study problems submitted to him and to make his recommendations by mail. Because of his intense love for our area he left the city of New Orleans only to travel to the Mississippi Gulf Coast where he kept his 28-foot sailboat, the *Nadia*.

Wood died at his favorite pastime, at the helm of his sailing vessel, leaving a will naming Tulane University, his alma mater, as recipient of all his wealth. There was only one condition: that *Nadia* be encased in glass for a period of 100 years.

Tulane University respected his wishes by constructing an indoor swimming pool with an adjacent glass-enclosed area where Wood's vessel can be seen for at least a century. In homage to this great man, the *Nadia* will surely be on display at his alma mater so long as there is a Tulane University.

And New Orleans will continue to revere him with high esteem as the man who made it possible for Orleanians to live in the "city below the sea" without having to grow gills.

CHAPTER SIX

*F*amous and Infamous Ladies of New Orleans

URSULINE NUNS:
The First Teachers and Nurses
of North America

In the 1720s the Company of the West (founded to administer the Louisiana Territory), through Father Beaubois, a Jesuit Priest in New Orleans, persuaded the Ursulines of Rouen, France, to establish a convent in Louisiana with a dual objective:

1. To educate the young girls.
2. To care for the sick.

The Ursulines graciously accepted the challenge. Mother Superior Tranchepain (an odd name for a nun—translated it means slice of bread) along with nine nuns, two postulants, one servant and a cat started on their journey to New Orleans.

The first leg of the trip was by stagecoach from Rouen to Lorient, with a side visit to the palace of the King at Versailles. Young Sister Madeline wrote home that while going through Versailles she considered shutting her eyes in fear of what she might see. Versailles at that time was renowned as a veritable palace of sin.

The ship scheduled to take them to their new home was the *Girondone.* Shortly after leaving port it struck a reef and narrowly escaped being shattered to pieces. This episode was just the first of a series of horrible events still in store. A terrible storm soon struck. The nuns were kept off the main deck in fear that they would be washed overboard. All of them were relegated to one small cabin and literally tied to the secured furniture so they would not be thrown about and injured seriously.

Soon after the first storm ended a second and more violent one enclosed the ship. It was so severe that all the livestock on board died from seasickness. For the passengers death would have been merciful, so debilitating was their trauma. After the big blow the nuns were slowly regaining strength and equilibrium when a pirate ship appeared menacingly off the stern. Although concerned, the captain showed enough firepower to drive away the threat. During the following month yet another storm, less severe than the first and second, hit the ship before it finally arrived at Santo Domingo and solid ground. As a special gift the people of Santo Domingo gave the nuns a barrel of much-treasured sugar.

The next leg of the journey was uneventful. From Santo Domingo to Dolphin Island the nuns were truly jubilant, but prematurely so; the vessel ran aground. Out came the rosaries. To reduce the weight of the ship the sugar had to be thrown overboard along with cannons and casks of liquor. Personal luggage was to be discarded next.

As the nuns said their rosaries the ship floated free and their belongings were spared. The ship finally reached the mouth of the Mississippi where nuns and luggage were loaded onto pirogues. Against the current they traveled toward their final destination, *La Nouvelle Orléans*.

Sister Madeline wrote that the five days on the Mississippi— perched atop luggage in unsteady pirogues, swatting mosquitos and looking out for snakes and alligators—were more tedious and treacherous than the seasickness of the storms and the threat of pirates.

In the early morning of August 7, 1727, exactly five months from the day they had left Rouen, France, the Ursulines reached the port city of New Orleans, mosquito bitten and weather-beaten, but happy to arrive in their new home. One young nun wrote home and gave the following first impression: "Upon seeing New Orleans for the first time, I can only say it looks like a large cesspool."

In their training the Ursuline Nuns had learned the meaning of hardship. In their trip from France they endured it and found yet more disappointments after arrival. Construction of the convent which had been pledged to them was scheduled to take six months to complete. Unfortunately, with New Orleans' proclivity for procrastination it took a total of seven years.

Reefs, storms, seasickness, pirates, mosquitos, snakes, alligators, construction delays and broken promises—none could deter the determined nuns who went on to accomplish their mission with dispatch and distinction.

DOROTHY DIX:
Premier Columnist

If it is true that the closest thing to gaining immortality is the written word Dorothy Dix will surely be remembered for all eternity. Her given name, Elizabeth Meriwether Gilmers, did not impress anyone. But her pen name, Dorothy Dix, would come to demand more attention than an E. F. Hutton television commercial.

At the turn of the century Dorothy Dix was recuperating from an illness when the manager of the *Picayune* newspaper asked if she would like to write a short story for publication. Her first contribution was sold to the daily for the grand sum of $3.00. It was so well received that she soon had a full-time job with the newspaper, where she began her famous column dispensing advice to the lovelorn.

Over the years many have copied her, but until this day Dorothy Dix's capability has never been matched; and her countrywide following on a per capita basis has probably never been equaled. By 1920 Dorothy Dix was the highest-paid woman writer in the world. Her column was carried by every major newspaper across the country and in many foreign lands.

For some strange reason on one of her world tours she purchased the bed of the scarlet and scandalous Madame Pompadour. Here was this grand dame of New Orleans society, a pillar of virtue, now owner of one of the most notorious beds to be found. She enjoyed telling her friends, "I'll bet I'm the only respectable woman who ever slept in it."

Who knows? By sleeping in Madame Pompadour's bed, Dorothy Dix might have received vibrations that guided her in giving advice to the lovelorn.

Myra Clarke Gaines spent nearly 65 years in court and finally won her "patrimony" case. (The Historic New Orleans Collection)

MYRA CLARK GAINES:
Persistence Personified

Daniel Clark, wealthy New Orleans landowner and one of Louisiana's leading political figures, was intimately acquainted with a man who would later become the King of France. And when Andrew Jackson came to New Orleans his first call was on Daniel Clark. However, while he rated highly with national and international leaders he was not at all well regarded by Louisiana Governor William C. C. Claiborne.

When the governor inferred that Clark might be involved in Aaron Burr's plot to overthrow the U.S. government a duel was scheduled. Pistols drawn, the two clashed at dawn. When the smoke cleared Claiborne lay sprawled on the ground with a bullet through the thigh. Clark had made his point.

When Clark died his will could not be located. The City of New Orleans contested the distribution of his estate, contending that his illegitimate daughter, Myra Clark Gaines, was not entitled to any of her father's vast resources.

Myra being the fighter that she was said, "We'll see!" and see they did. A series of her sensational lawsuits were featured in newspapers across America.

Myra's case was predicated on the term "Patrimony" (an estate inherited from one's father or ancestors). Lasting almost 65 years, the case went before the United States Supreme Court no less than twelve times. Testimony stretched to over 40,000 pages.

Myra Clark Gaines, "persistence personified," was before her death the ultimate winner. While legal fees left her with little in the way of funds, the victory left her with great satisfaction.

Myra, like so many of the greats in New Orleans' history, is buried in St. Louis No. 1 cemetery on world-renowned Basin Street.

MARGARET HAUGHERTY
First Statue Dedicated to a
Female in North America

Margaret Gafney Haugherty was destined to become one of New Orleans' best-loved women. She was born in County Caven, Ireland, and orphaned at nine when both of her parents died. She

moved shortly thereafter to the United States and was raised by a
non-relative, a Mrs. Richard. Margaret married Charles Haugherty and they made New Orleans their home. A beautiful daughter died soon after birth. After becoming ill, Charles embarked on
a voyage at sea in a futile effort to recuperate, but he also died.

Alone now Margaret was childless, widowed, uneducated
and untrained for any particular work. Although she had no experience in business, she started and built a very successful bakery
and devoted her life and profits to helping orphaned children. She
was successful in raising funds to erect St. Theresa's Asylum, and
once this establishment was operating to capacity, turned her at-
tentions and energies to helping the St. Vincent dePaul and St.
Elizabeth's asylums.

In 1882 Margaret died, having amassed an estate valued at
$30,000. All of it went to the New Orleans asylums, with equal
amounts to be allocated among the Catholic, Protestant and Jewish institutions.

As stated earlier, she was an uneducated person who signed
her will with an "X." But her funeral was one of New Orleans'
grandest and largest, attended by the governor, the mayor and
thousands upon thousands of grateful people whose lives she had
touched. When a marble statue was dedicated to Margaret in 1884
it was the first statue of a woman in all of North America.

To provide everyone an opportunity to contribute without
oversubscribing the cost of the statue no one was permitted to give
more than five cents. Still, the budget for the monument was easily raised.

The marble statue by Alexander Doyle still stands today on
a triangular piece of ground called Margaret's Place, surrounded
by Camp, Prytania and Clio Streets.

Margaret and her deeds were widely known, but a litany of
her good works will not be found on the statue. The simple inscription for this simple philanthropist is simply her first name,
Margaret.

MADAME LANGLOIS:
Mother of Creole Cooking

Shortly after New Orleans was founded in 1718 what may

The first statue dedicated to a female in North America was in tribute to New Orleans' own Margaret Haugherty. (Buddy Stall Collection)

have been the first protest in North America transpired because the women of the city knew little or nothing about indigenous foods. Instead of carrying picket signs they carried their black cast iron pots. Arriving at Governor Bienville's house they banged on the pots with utensils and insisted that he come out to hear their grievances.

Governor Bienville was not only a wise explorer and governor but also an outstanding diplomat. Seeing potential trouble looming ahead he agreed to send his housekeeper, Madame Langlois (a cousin of Bienville's mother) to live with the Indians for a period of approximately six weeks. By working with the Indians she discovered how they transformed native foods into delicious, digestible, and even delectable fare. She learned to use bay leaf to add flavor to foods, to make a meal from cut corn or to boil the ears whole. She found that the Indians would stuff squirrel with local pecans and spices, and the flavor was entrancing. Madame Langlois also became adept at preparing one of the better-known Indian dishes still appreciated today, corn and butterbeans melded to produce a dish we call "succotash." Upon her return she went about sharing her new-found knowledge with the ladies of New Orleans in what must have been the first home economics course to be held in North America.

Madame Langlois is today considered the Mother of Creole cooking.

MADAME LaLAURIE:
Socialite—Sadist

At 1140 Royal Street there stands today a magnificent home that was once the residence of a well-known and respected Creole named Madame LaLaurie. Prominent in New Orleans society and a beautiful woman, she was noted not only for her looks but for her charity and compassion on behalf of the less fortunate.

But looks can sometimes be deceiving. One evening, while Mr. and Mrs. LaLaurie were out at one of the gala events they liked to attend, a fire broke out at their residence and responding firemen were forced to break into the house. As fire fighters went through the structure they were aghast by what they discovered. In the attic they found several slaves, young boys and old men alike, chained in cells. In front of the cells was a long blood-stained table which was littered with instruments of torture. An old Negress, almost dead from starvation, was found in the kitchen. In another room were two black girls, more dead than alive and chained to cots. They too had been beaten and tortured. Their wounds were infected and they were no doubt being kept alive merely to prolong their suffering and to make them experience all that the most grotesque cruelty could inflict.

The fire drew the people of New Orleans like moths to a candle, and when they found out what had been happening inside the residence they became extremely angry. Mr. and Mrs. LaLaurie, in the meantime, had returned home and were quite disturbed to find out that their transgressions were no longer secret.

Mingling outside the smoldering house the crowd quickly turned into a mob. Fearing for their lives the LaLauries made a hasty exit via horse and carriage to Bayou St. John and headed for Mobile.

The mob eventually crashed into the house, released the chained victims and proceeded to loot and ransack the premises. Much of the furniture was broken, chairs and sofas were thrown through windows, and the magnificent mansion was left in shambles.

After the LaLauries eventually reached France rehashing of their perversions continued to circulate for decades. And the sounds of moans, cries and wailings are still reportedly heard in the still of the night at the "haunted house on Royal Street."

It is odd and incredible that Madame LaLaurie, on her deathbed in France, had the audacity to request in her final will and testament to be buried in New Orleans in St. Louis No. 1 Cemetery. She insisted that she had always considered New Orleans her home. The madame must have been deranged to want to be buried near the scene of her cruel crimes.

BARONESS PONTALBA:
Mover and Shaker

Micaela Pontalba's father, Baron Don Almonaster, a dynamic businessman and generous philanthropist, was 71 when he fathered her. After the Good Friday fire of 1788, when 862 struc-

tures burned to the ground, Baron Don Almonaster single-hand-
edly financed the reconstruction of the Cathedral, the Cabildo,
King's Hospital and the Hospital for Lepers.

On the other hand, he declined to pay for rebuilding the
Presbytere (Priest's house). The church bells had traditionally
served as the fire bells of the city but the pastor had refused to let
them ring so Almonaster was not anxious to do the clergymen any
favors.

Like her father, Micaela knew what she wanted and went after it. At fourteen she decided to marry her first cousin, Celestin
Pontalba. A special dispensation had to be obtained from the Pope
and she succeeded in her plea.

After marriage she moved to Paris with her new husband
where they lived in a magnificent chateau that is today the American Embassy. After three children—all sons—she sought a divorce, a most unusual request in those days. But Micaela was an
unusual lady. Her father-in-law protested violently; behind locked
doors in the study he took out a pistol and shot Micaela in the chest.
Luckily, she put one hand over her bosom, and although one of
her fingers was shot off, it deflected the bullet from her heart. She
then proceeded to take the gun away from her assailant, shot him
through the head and killed him instantly. Micaela recovered from
her wounds and obtained her divorce.

On her return to New Orleans, furious at seeing the Americans taking work away from the Creoles, she created jobs by building two apartment houses adjacent to *Place d'Armes*. Assisting architects James Gallier and Henry Howard in the design of the
structures, she was also responsible for supervising their construction. A shrewd businesswoman, she completed the second
building at a lower cost than the first. She also designed the grill-
work on the balconies in the shapes of A's and P's to represent her
maiden and married names, Almonaster and Pontalba.

Architects are still impressed with the design of the Pontalba
Apartments which draw convection currents from interior courtyards into the living units and out again to create an efficient ven-
tilation system.

As a prominent businesswoman Micaela was one of the New
Orleans delegates at the unveiling of the statue of her hero, Andrew Jackson, in Washington, D.C. On seeing it for the first time,

she wept openly and vowed to have one like it erected in New Orleans. Hastily returning to the city the Baroness launched a drive to raise sufficient funds. At the same time she sought authorization from the City Council to erect the statue in the square to be renamed in Jackson's honor. All necessary approval and sufficient funds were secured for the statue, and the square was renamed from *Place d'Armes* to Jackson Square. Until this day it carries that name. The Baroness was indeed a mover and shaker, and apparently, a good shot.

JOSEPHINE NEWCOMB:
Educator and Philanthropist

Paul Tulane (considered a most fastidious bachelor) was the founder of Tulane University (formerly the University of Louisiana). To its support he donated a half million dollars, and supposedly at his death he was to leave the balance of his vast fortune to this respected institution of higher learning. Upon his death in 1887 his will was never found and his estate went to others. But his university would continue to grow, thanks in part to a lady named Josephine Newcomb.

Mrs. Newcomb had only one daughter, Harriot Sophie Newcomb, who died at the tender age of 15. Greatly affected by her daughter's death, Josephine promptly donated in her memory a hundred thousand dollars to the Board of Administrators of Tulane University for the founding of a college for women.

Unlike Paul Tulane, Newcomb did leave a will. Her bequest to Newcomb College, the first women's institution in America operating under the auspices of a university, amounted to over three and a half million dollars. And that was in 1901, when a million dollars was worth a million dollars.

Although Josephine was small in stature, she was a giant in ability, achievement and generosity during her lifetime. And she was a giant in influence even after her death.

Over the years Newcomb College has distinguished itself in the arts, literature and music. When one of its students led the cheers for the Tulane football team it marked the first time a woman served as a cheerleader in America.

Josephine Newcomb deserves the cheers of thousands whose

lives have been enhanced through study at the oustanding institution she made possible.

MARIE LAVEAU:
Voodoo Queen

The last known witch of North America was a New Orleans mulatto named Marie Laveau. Her father, a wealthy white plantation owner named Charles Laveau, was also a member of the Louisiana Legislature.

Voodoo was brought to New Orleans and North America by the slaves from Africa and Haiti who were baptized Catholic by their Catholic masters because no other religion was allowed in Louisiana until after the Louisiana Purchase. Catholic or not, the slaves had deep religious roots and continued to practice voodoo, whether legal or not.

In a potpourri of rituals the slaves worshipped the Catholic's Virgin Mary alongside the snakes of the voodoo doctors. In their homes next to Catholic symbols, like statues of saints, blessed candles and holy water, could be found the entrails of toads and the claws of lizards.

Voodoo was practiced with fervor by slaves, free men of color, and even white men and women. Services included the drinking of large quantities of rum so that the liquid spirits might help one to see the invisible spirits of the voodoo god. Evidently, participants also smoked marijuana.

Marie, at age 36, married a freeman of color named Jacques Paris. When Jacques died Marie took up with a lover named Glapion, and apparently with the help of voodoo fertility potions, conceived and gave birth to fifteen children.

Marie started out as a hairdresser for the crème de la crème of New Orleans' society. In doing the hair of the beautiful ladies she found that they not only let their hair down but also confided their innermost feelings. As the confidant of the wealthy Marie got her start in the voodoo business. Soon she had all the customers she could handle.

One of Marie's strongest selling points was that she charged her clientele a great deal more than anyone else, thereby inferring that she was better at her craft than others. White clients paid $10.00

The best known voodoo queen in New Orleans history was one-time hairdresser Marie Laveau, shown with her daughter. (The Historic New Orleans Collection)

a visit . . . a tidy sum in her day. Once she worked for a well-to-do New Orleans couple whose son was in serious legal trouble. Marie, with some of her purported magic, worked wonders, because even though the young man was found guilty, the judge acquitted him. The father was so pleased he gave Marie a house on St. Ann Street. While Marie's expertise was potent in all areas of voodoo, her income came primarily from selling love potions. She lived in luxury to the ripe old age of 98 years.

Like many other famous and infamous women of New Orleans, Marie is buried in St. Louis No. 1 cemetery. People come from all over the world to visit her infamous tomb. It is said that if you want something from Marie simply make an "X" on her white tomb, and if you want something done to someone mark a double "XX." Perhaps it is an indication of the times we live in, but there are very few single "X's."

Someone jokingly said that Marie Laveau became the best-known voodoo queen, not because of the voodoo she learned from others but because her father was a Louisiana politician, and everyone knows that better con men cannot be found.

JOSIE ARLINGTON:
New Orleans' Number One Madam

The French law enacted at the behest of John Law made the technically-unemployed street women fair game for forced immigration to America. Therefore, the port city of New Orleans has been infested with prostitution from its very beginning.

Consequently, by the late 1880s prostitution was really running rampant with bordellos operating in almost every section of the city. A concerned political leader, a righteous man, took it upon himself to do research on means by which other port cities around the world were controlling this problem. He found the answer in the creation of "Red Light Districts" (red signifying danger). In these areas prostitution was regulated and supervised.

In 1898 a thirty-nine square-block area adjacent to downtown New Orleans and the Vieux Carré was established as the Red Light District and the approximately 3,800 prostitutes were forced to work in this newly-designated zone.

The most famous of all the Red Light District madams was

Miss Josie Arlington. As a young woman she stayed out one night later than allowed by her father and he literally locked her out of their home. Her boyfriend, a real loser, put her to work in the world's oldest profession.

When Josie died a beautiful marble tomb built at her request featured a statue of a young woman standing in front of her tomb and knocking symbolically at the door, just as Josie had knocked to no avail at the door of her home.

Shortly after being entombed someone with a bizarre sense of humor hung a red lantern from the hand of the statue, and it drew such crowds that a policeman had to be stationed in the area to keep the traffic moving. A New Orleans newspaper speculated that although Josie was now deceased she was still plying her trade.

CHAPTER SEVEN

*M*ardi *Gras/Other Special Events*

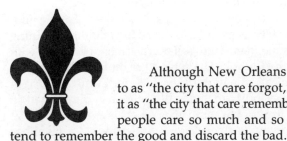

Although New Orleans is often referred to as "the city that care forgot," I like to think of it as "the city that care remembers," because our people care so much and so deeply. And we tend to remember the good and discard the bad.

We especially care profoundly about our world-famous period of celebration known as Carnival which culminates with Mardi Gras as its final crescendo. Beginning January and ending on the Tuesday (Mardi Gras is French for "Fat Tuesday") before Ash Wednesday, the weeks-long celebration is an integral part of the Crescent City psyche. Tied around the season of Lent and Easter, the observance actually began in pagan times as a time to petition the gods for fertile fields and fertile women.

Christianity soon recognized the intensity and fervor with which this period of feasting and frolicking was revered. Consequently, to attract converts, Christian leaders decided to initiate a rival period of fun and feasting in preparation for the somber season of Lent, a time of denial and reflection on the passion and crucifixion of Jesus Christ.

The Christian observance caught on and flourished as Christianity spread. When the French came to Louisiana in the early 1700s, Mardi Gras and its traditions came, too. While the customs that were being enjoyed in Catholic France were also practiced here, the fun-loving people of Louisiana refined and expanded the celebration. Instead of a one-day affair, the period of enjoyment eventually grew to weeks, its length depending on the dates of Easter Sunday and Ash Wednesday (six weeks earlier).

Today, it is not unusual to see a half million people at one of the Carnival parades, or twice that number, stacked like vertical French breads, trying to get a glimpse of Rex on Mardi Gras. During that crazy time of "not caring," one can witness revelers in all stages of dress and undress, and in every gradation of sobriety and less. Food and drink are consumed in mind-boggling quantities. Music fills the streets and ears of passers-by. Perfect strangers embrace passionately. Every means of self-gratification known to South Louisianians (and they are manifold) is indulged.

There was a time, before the 1960s, when the toll of the midnight bells on Mardi Gras meant the end of fun and the beginning of six weeks of fasting, denial and self-mortification. However, with the relaxation of the Catholic Church's rules on fasting and abstinence (of eating meat), the underlining alibi for Carnival—that of fattening up before the hard times of Lent—has diminished in prominence. But the annual romp goes on.

Instead of dying as a result of modifications, Carnival has grown by leaps and bounds during the past three or four decades. New Carnival krewes (clubs, organizations) have proliferated, some with startling success. The country and world are impressed with the growth of the festival in this international capital of Mardi Gras.

Tradition does not die hard in New Orleans. Rather, it grows easily. This one lives on and grows even more vigorously than ever.

Come to the Mardi Gras; you'll see.

The German Saengerbund

Hard-working German immigrants have been as important to our community as mortar is to a brick wall. In addition to a passion for production, the industrious Germans are also known for their passion for singing.

In the 1800s the New Orleans Chapter of the German Singing Society was considered the strongest of all similar associations from East Coast to West. As a result, the local organization was

chosen to host the national Saengerbund Singing Festival in our fair city. It was a big event for the German population.

A piece of land on the uptown/lake corner of Lee Circle was rented and a building was constructed at a cost of $50,000. Some called the structure striking, some amazing and others said it was nothing short of bizarre.

Measuring 95 feet wide and 40 feet high, the stage could hold up to 1,500 singers at a time and the music pit had room for 100 musicians. Since the entertainment was to be held on a continuous, 24-hour basis for four days and nights, special passages were designed so that singers and musicians could move about behind the scenes without disrupting those who were performing at the time.

Free of columns, the auditorium provided an unobstructed view of the stage from every one of the 4,056 seats which were completely filled for the duration.

At the conclusion of the marathon entertainment extravaganza the $50,000 facility was given to the Masonic Order by the generous Saengerbund. It was a sizable sum in those days to spend for four days of use, but the dedicated Germans had long before learned the hazards of all work and no play.

THE MARQUIS DE LAFAYETTE/
ARC DE TRIOMPHE

New Orleans has always had a flair for welcoming special guests to the city and the reception of Marie Joseph Paul Yves Roch Gilbert du Motier, Marquis de Lafayette, was no exception. Although he had declined the invitation to be the state's first governor when the United States purchased Louisiana, his popularity had not diminished.

In preparation for his visit the city government decided to go to extremes befitting a Frenchman of such rank. The famous and much-used city hall, the Cabildo, was emptied completely of its contents and redecorated as Lafayette's residence for his six-day visit. From this vantage point he would be able to view and appreciate the surprise planned for *Place d'Arms* (later Jackson Square) in his honor.

A noted military leader who had so greatly aided the Americans in their fight for freedom, Lafayette was greeted at the site of the Battle of New Orleans in Chalmette by Louisiana Governor Henry S. Johnson and other leading citizens of the state. From there a large parade made its way into the city where an anxious and enormous crowd was waiting patiently with New Orleans Mayor Louis Philippe de Roffignac, who was to officially welcome the Marquis de Lafayette to the city.

When the parade, headed by the Marquis came into view, church bells began pealing as the horde waved handkerchiefs and chanted, *"Vive Lafayette, vive Lafayette."* The closer he came the louder they cheered, and the more enthusiastically they waved their handkerchiefs. When the Marquis reached *Place d'Arms*, what seemed like a battalion of cannons fired in salute. Here on foreign soil he was being treated like a demigod.

In tribute City Engineer J. Pilie had been instructed by city fathers to design a replica of the *Arc de Triomphe*. The 68-foot high, 58-foot wide, 25-foot deep replica, painted to look like green marble, was constructed by J. B. Fogliardi. On the base were painted figures representing justice and liberty. Adorning the Arch were two allegorical forms with trumpets and ribands depicting fame and bearing the names of Washington and Lafayette. At the very top was a statue representing wisdom above a bust of Benjamin Franklin.

Mayor Roffignac was standing under the Arch ready to welcome Lafayette to the city but the clapping and the shouting was deafening. So, he simply pointed to an inscription which read in both French and English, "A grateful republic consecrates this monument to Lafayette."

The 68-year-old Marquis de Lafayette, immortal French patriot and hero of three revolutions, was treated in the manner New Orleans felt he deserved.

Out of sight, out of mind did not hold true in his case; he was not forgotten after his visit in 1825. Three Faubourgs (subdivisions), Annunciation, Livaudais and Lafayette, were incorporated in 1833 by a legislative act as the City of Lafayette. Lafayette consisted of 14,000 people, a cemetery, railway, newspaper, fire department and its own still-existent Lafayette Square, located directly across from the old City Hall (now called Gallier Hall).

The City of Lafayette was finally absorbed into the city of New

Marie Joseph Paul Yves Roch Gilbert du Motier, Marquis de Lafayette. (The Historic New Orleans Collection)

To show their affection for the great French military leader Marquis de Lafayette, who visited New Orleans in 1825, city fathers erected a 65-foot-high replica of the *Arc de Triomphe* in *Place d'Arms* (now Jackson Square). (The Historic New Orleans Collection)

Orleans in 1852 but, as if in recompence, the name of Vermilion City in Southwest Louisiana was changed to the City of Lafayette, which is now the oil capital of Louisiana.

THE MOST ELABORATE NEGRO FUNERAL
EVER HELD IN NEW ORLEANS

Major Adolphe J. Osey was a man who believed in belonging to numerous lodges. He was founder of several and served as a high dignitary in almost all of them at one time or other.

Because of the multitude of organizations to which he belonged, his death notice in the newspaper was one of the longest on record:

> OSEY—At his residence, 2311 Upperline Street, Tuesday, July 20, 1937, at 11:55 o'clock p.m., MAJOR ADOLPHE J. OSEY, a native of Bellalliance, Louisiana, and a resident of this city for many years. Beloved husband of Henrietta Webb Osey, grandfather of Oscar J. Osey, uncle of Emanuel, Jr., Edgar Porter, Eddie and Joseph Howard, Manuella Porter McCleanton, Henrietta Webb Gumbs, Ethel Howard McTurner, great-uncle of Nellie Porter Walker, James and Juanita Porter, brother-in-law of John Webb and Emanuel B. Porter, and a host of other relatives.
>
> Grand Staff Patriot, 13th Regiment of G.U. of O. of America, Louisiana Creole Lodge, G.U.O. of O.F. 1918, Past Grand Masters Council No. 30, Esther H.H. of Ruth No. 3964, Cyprus Lodge, A.A. & F.M. No. 43, Capitol Lodge of Elks No. 595, Progressive Friends Ben. Ass., Young Men's Perpetual Hel. Ben. Ass. Live Wire Circle of 5th Baptist Church, Star Light Circle of Tulane Baptist Church, Pastor, officers and friends of Trinity M.E. Church are respectfully invited to attend the funeral, which will take place from the late residence, Sunday, July 25, 1937, at 11:30 o'clock a.m.
>
> Religious services 5th Baptist Church, Sixth and South Robertson Streets.
>
> Reverend W. B. McClelland Officiating.
> Interment St. Louis Cemetery No. 23

Major Osey was laid out in his four-room cottage located at 2311 Upperline Street. The front door was draped with a dark canopy of black velvet, edged with silver fringe. His casket was of

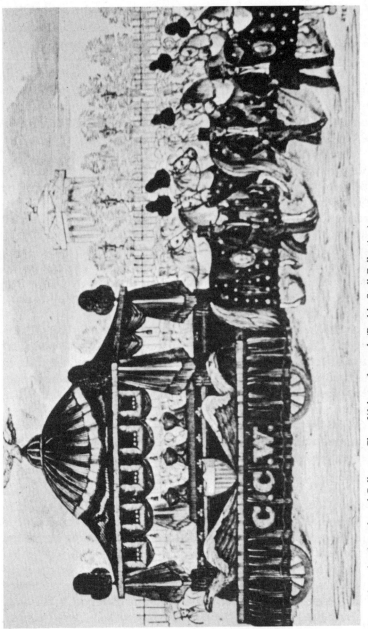

Funeral car for the colossal Calhoun, Clay, Webster funeral. (Buddy Stall Collection)

plush purple with a lining of light blue silk. A bed light attached to the coffin lid illuminated his face, which was fixed with a smile so wide that all his pearly teeth could be seen. (They were his own and he had been proud of them.)

It was Osey's wish that he be as impartial in death as he had been in life. He was dressed in a jet-black Odd Fellows uniform with polished brass buttons and shining gold braid. Around his waist was the lambskin of the Supreme Masons Council. His white-gloved hands held a purple fez of the Elks.

Upon the "joiner's" chest were medals of the past grand council encampment of the past patriarch, signifying, according to one member, that Major "was really in the groove." On top of the coffin were a Bible, the Elks Sphere, brass buttons from the Progressive French, an Odd Fellows rosette and a small Mason's wreath.

The funeral procession was led by the 6'3" jet-black Grand Marshall of the Odd Fellows, followed by his clan, keeping perfect time to the slow, stomp-swinging music of a 13-piece band. The marchers wore black and gold uniforms, plumed hats and yellow gloves.

Next came shiny limosines from the various lodges, followed by a legion of mournful marchers dressed in a wide spectrum of colorful uniforms. (Ladies' auxiliaries were also there to march in tribute.) The last three Odd Fellows carried a gilded lion, a lamb and a bow and arrow, the significance of which was a lodge secret.

In the last limosine could be seen a statue of Father Time equipped with gold wings and a smile on its whiskered countenance. Dressed in scarlet pants, the statue held an hourglass and a scythe.

Total distance from the home of the deceased to the Fifth Baptist Church and then to the cemetery was five miles.

Some 21 well-known participants from lodges, churches, and singing groups offered remarks, prayers, condolences, songs and sermons. It was a marathon of a burial service.

With services finally over, Odd Fellows crossed swords as the coffin was taken back to the limosine. The funeral then proceeded to St. Louis No. 2 Cemetery where a burial dialogue, particularly praising the late Major's tongue, cheeks, eyes and nose ensued, followed with the placing of a bouquet of evergreens within the vault. After Mrs. Patterson rendered a solo titled "The Will of God is Accomplished," mourners paid their last respects by throwing handfuls of ashes into the tomb.

As the throng left the cemetery the bands changed their tunes from mournful to joyful and the marchers began to dance in the street in celebration of another soul's entrance into heaven. In high spirits and swaying cadence they headed back to Major Osey's house to hold a party commemorating the exit of a good member who could not be accused of discrimination.

New Orleans prosperity returns to the port after the Civil War. (The Historic New Orleans Collection)

CHAPTER EIGHT

*S*teamboats

The steamboat would have to be credited with making New Orleans one of the leading ports in the United States before the Civil War; at that time it was second and striving to be first. Unfortunately, the Civil War came and the economy of the South was depressed for decades. But today, with exploding commerce on the lower Mississippi, New Orleans has become the leading port in the country and is surpassed in the world only by the port of Amsterdam, Holland.

The steamboat literally introduced the "boom" era on the lower Mississippi as hundreds of steamboats exploded, caught fire and often sank from the mishaps. Metalurgy was not what it is today and captains were not as concerned with safety.

Plying the interstates, highways and rural roads of its day— namely rivers, lakes and bayous—the steamboat brought freight, passengers, entertainment and prosperity to an immobile society.

While the man responsible for inventing the steamboat was Robert Fulton, the one responsible for making the Mississippi River safe for travel was Captain Henry Miller Shreve (Shreveport, La. is named in his honor). He actually built the first steamboat that could go upriver carrying a full load and still travel into the shallow bayous of the Pelican State to deliver supplies to many areas previously inaccessible by steamboat. Captain Shreve was also responsible for designing, building, and using the first snag boat with which he cleared the Red River to the point that commerce was once again free to move on this great waterway.

Captain Shreve also has two other distinctions. His first vessel, the *Enterprise,* was the first steamboat to be used in warfare at the Battle of New Orleans. The other is the fact that when Shreve designed his steamboat he named rooms on board after states; hence the name "stateroom."

The following covers just a few of the unusual and exciting happenings involving steamboats, including the first steamboat ever to come down the mighty Mississippi, the worst marine disaster of all time and the world's greatest steamboat race.

NEW ORLEANS—THE FIRST STEAMBOAT TO DESCEND THE MISSISSIPPI

The first steamboat to descend the Mississippi and dock in New Orleans arrived on January 12, 1812. It was appropriately called *New Orleans.*

Mastering the Mississippi was an idea conceived by Robert Fulton and Robert Livingston after the successful voyage of their steamboat, *Clermont,* in 1807. Having acquired a monopoly on steamboat operations in New York, the two fancied a similar situation on the Mississippi. In May, 1809, Fulton hired Nicholas Roosevelt, an engine builder, to survey the mighty river and produce a feasibility study on the potential venture.

Roosevelt was a man of extraordinary skills and knowledge. He not only surveyed the river, he also solved the problem of energy needs by lining up sources of coal along the way. Seven months later the survey was completed, on December 1, 1809, and Roosevelt booked passage for the voyage back to New York to make his favorable report. Yellow fever broke out on board and many died. Roosevelt was removed from the steamer by a pilot craft and completed the trip by stagecoach. His positive report impressed Fulton and Livingston, who could see vast wealth in controlling the economy of the Mississippi River Valley.

Roosevelt and his wife established residence in the frontier town of Pittsburgh in the spring of 1811. At Beelens Iron Foundry the keel for a steamboat was laid according to Fulton's plans. It was

The record load of 9,226 cotton bales, loaded in New Orleans on the Steamboat *Henry Frank*, April 2, 1881, still stands as an all-time record. (The Historic New Orleans Collection)

to be 148½ feet long and 32½ feet wide with a draft of 12 feet. The engine was to have a 34-inch cylinder. When work was well underway flood waters of the Monongahela River floated shipyard equipment to all points of the compass. Through superhuman efforts the job was finished, and in September of 1811 the boat christened *New Orleans* was ready for its trial run. When people heard that the *New Orleans* planned to travel upriver, as well as down, skeptics thought the idea was absurd.

On October 1 the *New Orleans* reached Louisville. A large crowd had gathered—but not to see the boat. The comet of 1811 had been in the heavens and sounds of the steam engine attracted multitudes who thought the comet had fallen into the Ohio River and was making a sizzling sound. Roosevelt was honored with a dinner ashore, and as usual, doubts concerning his going upriver against the current were expressed. On the next evening Roosevelt had a dinner on board for honored guests, and while they were enjoying the meal engines were started and the steamboat left its moorage. When guests reached topside they were dumbfounded to find the boat going upstream against the current! Doubting Thomases became instantaneous believers.

The real danger facing Roosevelt was not the current but the falls ahead. With the Ohio River at its lowest level Roosevelt killed time by carrying unbelievers upriver to Cincinnati to prove that upstream trips were feasible. Finally, the day of reckoning was at hand. Two extra pilots who knew the falls inside and out were engaged. As the boat entered the abyss it dipped into eddy-swirling water. Spray whipped the decks and the engine roared. As if stabilized by a giant gyroscope she spun around and righted herself. The vessel pitched to what seemed certain destruction but bobbed up again. Finally over the ordeal, the *New Orleans* landed safely below the rapids.

There was little time for rejoicing. As the *New Orleans* tied up the world seemed to tear itself at the seams. The ground heaved and shook: water rushed from bank to bank and at one point even flowed upstream! The strongest earthquake to ever affect the North American Continent—the New Madrid tragedy of 1811—struck at the same time, as though it resented the intrusion of steam's challenge of the Mississippi. Roosevelt and the *New Orleans* rode out the night of horror and only through great effort was his boat kept on an even keel. Although the rumbling from the earthquake continued throughout the next day, Roosevelt mustered up enough steam and the boat raced downriver. When the *New Orleans* stopped for fuel, riverbank inhabitants pleaded to be taken away from the destruction of the earthquake.

Beyond the falls and the earthquake were the Indians. Shouting war hoops they tried to attack the spark-spitting monster they thought was responsible for making the ground shake. As arrows were scraped from the hull a servant in the forward cabin inadvertently started a fire. Before it could be extinguished a sizable amount of damage had resulted, but still the *New Orleans* headed to her destination of the Crescent City. Upon seeing the steamboat for the first time a black man on the bank was said to have thrown his hat in the air and shouted, "Ole Mississippi done got her master now."

Neither falls, nor earthquake, Indians or fir a could stop the craft. The balance of the trip was without incident. The first steamboat to reach the Port of New Orleans arrived on January 2, 1812. Thereafter used in New Orleans-to-Natchez trade, the *New Orleans* established the Fulton-Livingston claim to their monopoly.

In operation until July 13, 1814, the historic vessel hit a submerged stump near Baton Rouge. Trying to break loose she took on water and sank to the bottom of the river. Gone, but not forgotten!

STEAMBOAT *LOUISIANA;* BARELLI CHILD

Along with prosperity to New Orleans, steamboats also brought despair, grief, and misery. Captain John W. Cannon, who was later victorious in the great steamboat race between the *Robert E. Lee* and the *Natchez* in 1870, owned a steamboat named *Louisiana.* She was scheduled to dock on November 18 between the steamboats *Bostona* and *Storm* at the foot of Gravier Street. After discharging her passengers, the *Louisiana* was scheduled to pick up 200 German immigrants below Esplanade Avenue. With his wife, Joseph Barelli, a leading Italian merchant, president and a founder of the New Orleans Italian Mutual Benevolent Society, disem-

The most publicized steamboat race of all time, the *Natchez* versus the *Robert E. Lee*, began on June 30, 1870. The *Robert E. Lee* left the *Natchez* in its smoke soon after the 5:00 p.m. starting gun was fired. (The Historic New Orleans Collection)

barked at Gravier Street. However, they permitted their young son to ride on to Esplanade Avenue where they would pick him up in their buggy.

At exactly 5:00 p.m. on Thursday, November 19, 1849, the steamboat *Louisiana* blew her boiler. The steamboats *Bostona* and *Storm* docked next to her were instantly leveled to the water line. Blown 50 feet out into the river, the *Storm* sank immediately. People standing as far as 200 feet from the wharf were mowed down by debris. A mule was cut in half by flying shrapnel. One piece of metal was propelled five blocks away to Canal and Front streets where it completely leveled a popular coffee house. On the *Louisiana* a man standing on deck above the boiler received not a scratch, yet people in all directions were either killed or severely injured.

Every house in New Orleans shook. Hospitals and graveyards added scores to their rolls. In all it is estimated 86 people were killed and untold numbers were injured. Luckily the steamboat *Storm* had just unloaded all of her passengers upriver at the City of Lafayette.

The body of the Barelli's son was never found. His bereaved father dedicated a monument to his memory which stands to this day in St. Louis No. 2 Cemetery. Surrounded by five large praying angels, a chiseled scene in the tomb portrays the explosion and the sinking of the *Louisiana* as the spirit of the Barelli boy is lifted by angels into heaven.

THE GREAT RACE

Surely, the greatest steamboat race ever held began in New Orleans on June 30, 1870. The race was staged between two captains who were once business partners but in time became bitter enemies.

Captain Thomas Paul Leathers of the Steamboat *Natchez* had shaved one hour and twelve minutes off the New Orleans-to-St. Louis record. Captain John W. Cannon was, to say the least, furious! Although a Yankee, he christened his new steamboat the *Robert E. Lee* because it was operating in Southern waters.

A short time after Captain Cannon put the *Lee* into service he and Captain Leathers had a violent argument which led to a fist fight that culminated into an organhead (a riverman's word for bet).

The two agreed to a race from New Orleans to St. Louis. Wagering on a Super Bowl, Kentucky Derby and a Louisiana gubernatorial election all rolled into one might have equaled the volume of betting for the big race.

The big day finally arrived. Both boats were tied up at the Canal Street landing ready for the 5:00 p.m. starting gun. Boilers were stoked with fat pine knots, and hundreds of pounds of salt meat were on board to generate superheated steam.

By starting time wagering had taken on local, state, national and international dimensions. This was indeed *The Great Race!*

Easing away from the landing the vessels were belching smoke and spewing sparks as they headed for the starting point at St. Mary's market.

At exactly 5:00 p.m. the starting gun sounded and they were off. While photographs of the great race show the two contestants head to head, it was only at the start that these pictures could have been taken. When the *Natchez* reached the Carrollton bend the *Lee* was out of sight. By the time they reached Baton Rouge the *Lee* was nine miles ahead. Upon reaching Vicksburg, Miss. the leader tied up at midstream alongside a faster steamboat and refueled. Bettors cried foul, but the race went on.

Captain Cannon and the *Robert E. Lee* carried no freight and only a small select number of passengers while Captain Leathers carried full freight and a full passenger list. When the *Robert E. Lee* encountered heavy upriver shoal waters and heavy fog she took on experienced pilots and kept on steaming, while the *Natchez* tied up until the fog had lifted.

On July 4, 1870, the *Robert E. Lee* arrived in St. Louis with a new record time of three days, 18 hours and 13 minutes, having shattered the previous record by three hours and 56 minutes.

Fueled by this entry into the "rapid" transit era, the Fourth of July celebration in St. Louis was one to remember. On the other hand, Captain Leathers' dismal defeat may have given "birth to the blues." Today, a new steamboat named after his *Natchez* plies the waters of the Mississippi River around New Orleans.

Captain Cannon didn't make any money on that trip but his new record generated business galore.

Ironically, on June 30, 1896, famous Captain Leathers, then

The 1,547 deaths resulting from the *Sultana*'s explosion still represent the world's greatest marine tragedy. (The Historic New Orleans Collection)

80 years old but still as tough as river leather, was killed in New Orleans on St. Charles Avenue by a hit and run bicycle rider.

THE FLAMING COFFIN:
WORLD'S GREATEST MARINE TRAGEDY

In April 1865 the great steamboat *Sultana* pulled out of New Orleans for Cairo, Ill. Her mission of mercy was to pick up Union prisoners along the way and return them to their homes. But death was stalking the *Sultana*. Licensed to carry 376 people, including the crew, she began picking up wounded and weary Union prisoners along the river.

Hasty repairs were made to a leaking boiler because no one wanted to delay the prisoners any longer than necessary. But when the *Sultana* reached Vicksburg, Miss. the leak was evident again. Jammed on her decks was a total of 2,500 men plus the crew . . . almost seven times as many as the steamer's capacity.

The clerk of the *Sultana* told one soldier, "If the boat arrives safely at Cairo, and I have serious doubts that it will, it will be the greatest trip ever made on Western waters."

On April 25, 1865, the *Sultana* docked at Helena, Ark. A photographer took a picture of the human cargo that would later be printed in newspapers around the world. On the very next night, while taking on coal from a barge in midstream, the boiler exploded. In 20 minutes the ship was completely engulfed in flames; hence the name given to this ghastly tragedy, "The Flaming Coffin." Shrieks, moans, cries for mercy . . . the gnashing of teeth permeated the darkness. Mangled and burned bodies were stacked six deep. The tragedy was compounded by a driving rain, a swift current and a wide river approaching flood stage.

When the catastrophe was over and those who survived had been collected the death count stood at 1,547. What had started out as a mission of mercy concluded in a nightmare of misery in the greatest marine tragedy ever recorded.

CHAPTER NINE

New Orleans' 1884 World's Fair

In 1862 New Orleans became the first major city in the Confederacy to fall to Federal troops and to be occupied.

After the Civil War ended in 1865 New Orleans was controlled by a corrupt carpet-bag government. It was not until 1877, when radical Republican Governor Stephen B. Packard was defeated, that the terrible era of reconstruction came to an end. Louisiana was, therefore, under occupation longer than any other Confederate State.

For 15 tough, long, lean years, New Orleans was prostituted in every imaginable way. The economy of the city, like most of the cities in the South, was in shambles.

But the people of New Orleans have always been noted for bouncing back . . . . after a hurricane, a flood, fire, yellow fever epidemic, a Civil War or the usual New Orleans Saints football season. By 1880 our community was beginning to feel its oats once again. Business, civic and political leaders were pulling together to light a flame under the economy of "the New South."

At the annual meeting of the National Cotton Planters Association in October of 1882, it was suggested a celebration be planned for the 100th anniversary of cotton as the leading southern industry. The first recorded shipment of cotton from North America to the world's markets was from Charlotte, North Carolina to England in 1784. While the first shipment amounted to only six bags, it was an officially-recorded shipment. In only one century shipments of cotton from North America to world markets increased four-million-fold to an annual volume of seven million bales and became the leading export.

While there were those who were enthusiastic and fervently in favor of a large celebration, the faint-hearted sour-graped the idea and kept the matter in abeyance for months. But southern men of vision would not let a few dissenters dampen their enthusiasm. They soon convinced the Congress of the United States to adopt an act creating the World's Industrial and Cotton Centennial of 1884, and naturally the world's leading cotton port was chosen as the host of the fair.

The specific site chosen was Upper City Park (now Audubon Park) on some 249 acres of level land right on the Mississippi River. It was felt that the river would make the fair accessible to 20,000 miles of navigable streams. In addition, the Mississippi to the Gulf was now in full service since Captain James B. Eads had completed his jetties at the mouth of the river. This new structure would allow the largest ships in existence to travel upstream, dock alongside the park and unload freight and passengers within a few feet of the fairgrounds.

Besides water transportation, rails made New Orleans accessible to all states and territories in the U.S., Mexico and Canada.

Chosen to run the fair were men whose names might today raise an eyebrow or two. The treasurer's last name was Lafitte (New Orleans previously had a famous pirate by that name). The secretary was Richard Nixon (probably no relation to the ex-President).

The real fly in the organizational ointment was Major Edward A. Burk, Director General and Treasurer of Louisiana. Burk was a master politician, a pre-destined leader with a combative instinct bent upon conquering. When offered the job for $55,000 he rose to his feet. Those who had made the offer were fearful they might have offended him by not offering enough. Instead he said:

> I graciously accept, but I cannot accept $55,000 for this job. I will take only $5,000 and assure you I can and will make a success of this project. I recommend you share the $50,000 balance equally with the ten universities within the city limits of New Orleans.

Shortly after the 1884 World's Fair ended, both the Director General, Major E. A. Burke, and $1,777,000 of state funds vanished. (The Historic New Orleans Collection)

Major Burk ran the fair with determination but not as successfully as he had hoped. Shortly after the exposition concluded he could not be found anywhere in the city nor in the State of Louisiana. In fact he was not even in the United States. It turned out he was living in France, and when asked by telegram for an accounting of his stewardship (and $1,777,000), he declined and moved to Central America where he and all of the proceeds from the 1884 World's Fair and some state funds were dedicated to building a large plantation where he lived out the rest of his life. The *Picayune* newspaper ran an article regarding this unfortunate debacle stating, "The collapse of the World's Cotton and Industrial Centennial Exposition signed the death warrant of any other such enterprise thereafter forever in New Orleans."

A century later the newspaper would be proven wrong.

Forever is a long time and just as Orleanians are quick to bounce back, they are also people who are quick to forgive and forget. New Orleans hosts its second world's exposition in 1984, one hundred years after the city's first fair.

Although it was a financial disaster, the fair of 1884 brought economical and educational bonanzas for New Orleans and the entire South. Its value in resurrecting the city and the region can never be estimated in mere dollars and cents. It no doubt produced a positive frame of mind for the resilient populace.

THE MAIN BUILDING AND
THE GRAND OPENING OF THE FAIR

For the World Industrial and Cotton Centennial to give "the New South" slogan meaning and impact organizers left no stone unturned.

Every state and territory agreed to have an exhibit. All major foreign countries were contacted, again with great results. France, Italy, Great Britain, Austria, Russia, Germany, Denmark, Japan, Portugal and Spain were among the nations agreeing to participate. Major countries also consented to display some of their cherished art treasures in a fireproof iron and glass Art Gallery that would cover one and a quarter acres.

The 1884 exposition had a total of 81 acres under roof, almost 10 percent more than any previous fair.

The Main Building of the 1884 World's Fair enclosed 33 acres, thus covering almost four times as much area as the present-day Louisiana Superdome. (The Historic New Orleans Collection)

The permanent structure of the fair would be a glass Horti-cultural Hall that would cover three-and-a-half acres to house gardens from all continents of the world. Fresh fruit and flowers would be brought in for display and consumption. In spite of all of these outstanding features the greatest attraction would be the Main Building. Designed to be larger than any previous World's Fair building, it still holds that distinction today. Simply called the Main Building, it measured 1,378 feet long by 905 feet wide. It had no partitions and the pillars supporting the roof structure were set widely apart, thereby presenting no obstruction to vision. The design aided the viewer in absorbing the vast size of the rambling building. As big as it was, one could stand in a corner of the second level and see clear across to the opposite corner without interference.

Compared to the Louisiana Superdome, which covers nine acres, the Main Building covered 33 acres under roof and was, therefore, almost four times as large in area covered as the Superdome.

In 1884 the City of New Orleans had only 482 light bulbs. The Main Building had 5,000, and needless to say, the array of illumination presented one of the highlights. Glass skylights also let in an abundance of light without subjecting the interior to the direct rays of the sun.

Designed to house foreign agricultural machinery and general exhibits, the huge structure had in its center a Music Hall with a seating capacity of 11,000 and a stage that could accommodate 600 musicians and singers. Those who attended the daily performances in the Music Hall were treated to the luxuries of cushioned armed chairs, electric illumination, electric fans and accoustical excellence.

If a visitor wanted to see all that was happening in the Main Building at one time he could take one of the 20 safety appliance electric elevators to the spacious galleries above the main floor. From there he could scan two miles of steel shafting that was turning and operating a diverse variety of new machines known to man. For a bird's eye view of the 249 acres of the fair the Observation Tower could be reached again by electric elevator where one could get an eyeful that would last, as advertised, "for a lifetime."

The Louisiana Superdome. (Louisiana Tourist Commission)

The Grand Opening

Proclamation by the President of the United States of America:

And whereas the fully constituted board of managers of the aforesaid World's Industrial and Cotton Centennial Exposition has informed me that provision has been made for the erection of suitable buildings for the purpose of the said exposition.

Now, therefore, I, Chester A. Arthur, President of the United States of America, by authority of and in fulfillment of the requirements of said Act, approved February 10, 1883, do hereby declare and make known that the World's Industrial and Cotton Centennial Exposition will be opened on the first Monday in December, 1884, at the City of New Orleans, in the State of Louisiana and will there be held continuously until the 31st day of May, 1885.

In witness whereof, I have hereunto set my hand and caused the Seal of the United States to be affixed.

Done at the City of Washington this 10th day of September, 1883 and of the Independence of the United States in the 108th.

Chester A. Arthur
President of the United States

When the first Monday in December, 1884, came around the fairgrounds were far from being completed and the official opening date was set back to December 16 so that the Main Building, where the ceremonies were to take place, could be completed.

On December 16 carpenters and other craftsmen were still working frantically. But the opening took place anyway. Considering the fact that the Main Building was approximately four times larger than the Superdome and was completed in a little over six months it was truly an engineering feat. (It took over seven years to build the Louisiana Superdome.) Consider also that the fireproof Art Gallery was completed in only five-and-a-half weeks, and the 12-acre Government Building was completed in only two and a half months.

As previously stated, nothing of importance can begin in our city without a parade, and this was no exception. From the St. Charles Hotel in the 200 block of St. Charles Street the procession moved down Canal Street and to the river. The electrified, enthusiastic crowd waited patiently for a chance to see the big names taking part in the parade. A Mexican band led the march and was followed by immaculately-dressed Mexican soldiers. Then came local military units which were followed by numerous dignitaries, including Louisiana Governor Samuel Douglas McEmery and hosts of local, state and federal officials, diplomats from foreign countries, Indian chiefs from numerous tribes throughout the United States, military officers, clergymen and prominent local citizens.

When they arrived at the river the decorated steamboat *Fred A. Banks* was awaiting them for an upriver parade to the exposition grounds. Just a few hundred yards from her docking berth the *Banks* passed the French Man of War, *Bovet*, which fired a salute and proceeded to escort the *Banks* upriver with several other crowded steamers following in their wake. At 12:20 p.m., the Washington Artillery, in formation on the levee, fired a salute announcing their arrival to the 12,000 people already assembled in the Main Building.

Rumor had spread that Jefferson Davis, former President of the Confederacy, would make a surprise appearance. Instead, ex-governor Alexandre Mouton, the state's first Creole governor, was on board, but while he was a great Creole gentleman he was not a man of Jefferson Davis' stature.

As the dignitaries disembarked they were led to the Music Hall by yet another parade, this one led by the Mexican Cavalry Band, and upon reaching the hall music continued within, courtesy of the Curriers Cincinnati Band.

Everyone was now seated and the stage was filled to capacity with 600 musicians and singers. Decorated with flags and bunting, the building conveyed an atmosphere that was nothing short of magnetizing.

The opening ceremony began with the playing of the specially-written Exposition Grand March followed by an invocation by the Reverend T. DeWitt Talmadge, a noted nineteenth century minister, who said, "Gracious God, through this exposition, solve for us the agonizing question of supply and demand." Major Burk then introduced Edmund Richardson, president of the Board of Managers of the fair, who delivered a speech that was relayed by telegraph to President Chester Arthur in the East Room at the White House.

Chester Arthur answered with a telegraphed speech of his own and at 2:11 p.m. New Orleans time he pushed a button which rang a bell in the large Music Hall authorizing H. W. Burr, an exposition engineer, to activate the 650-horsepower engine generating the electricity for the fair. As the engine started up 5,000 bulbs showered light throughout the building, electric fans whirred and the shafts of the turning machinery in the Main Building made music of their own. With power the electric train and electric streetcars on the grounds were now operative and waiting to serve the people.

When the crowd finally quieted down after the magnificent electrical display, Burk's small son raised a hugh portrait of President Chester Arthur. The audience cheered as the Washington Artillery fired continuous salvos followed by rounds of salute from the French Warship *Bovet*.

As the crowd settled down, New Orleans' Mayor H. V. Guillotte, spoke: "The sea of faces that surround me has almost overcome me. Consequently, I crave your indulgence of the brevity of my remarks," which were over in one minute.

Next to the podium was Louisiana Governor S. D. McEmery who, unlike Mayor Guillotte, rendered a typical Louisiana political speech—very long and apparently, very boring.

Finally, the climax of the evening was a reading by Major P. M. Baker of a poem especially written for the occasion by Mary Ashley Townsend, a wealthy New Orleans eccentric. "The Centennial Poem" was of epic length and was a valiant attempt to capture the spirit of the Cotton Industrial Centennial.

NEW ORLEANS AT THE TIME
OF THE 1884 WORLD'S FAIR

A look at New Orleans in 1884.

POPULATION—250,000 (estimated), ranking tenth in population in the United States.

LAND AREA—155 square miles, largest city in the world, with six square miles more than London. Over seven times the area of New York and 26 square miles larger than Philadelphia.

STREETS—650 miles lighted by 4,599 gas lamps, 2,000 oil lamps and 482 electric lights.

WEATHER—the average temperature in New Orleans from December to May: 65 degrees.

HOTELS—13 with total capacity of 4,250 guests (average cost: $3.00 a day). Two new hotels under construction in the area of the fair grounds with a total capacity of 2,000 people.

BOARDING HOUSES AND LODGING HOUSES—over 2,000 with accommodations ranging from 10 to 40 persons each (cost: $1.00 to $2.00 per day).

NEWSPAPERS

Bee (French)	5 cents
City Item	5 cents
Evening Chronicle	5 cents
German Gazette	5 cents
Picayune	5 cents
States	5 cents
Times Democrat	5 cents
Morning Star	5 cents
Mascot	5 cents
Figaro (illustrated)	10 cents

COLLEGES

University of Louisiana
University of Louisiana Medical Department
University of Louisiana Law Department
Louisiana College of Pharmacy
Jefferson College
Jesuits College
Soules College
Southern University
Straight University
Valence Institute

TRANSIT TO THE FAIR—New Orleans boasted the finest and most efficient transit system in the United States. Six street railroad departures ran from Canal Street to the fairgrounds every 30 minutes and ran into an elegant depot at the grounds.

Street railways also traveled throughout the city.

PUBLIC PLEASURE VEHICLES—(hacks, carriages and cabs). Fixed rates were to be posted in all public pleasure vehicles. Rates applied from sunrise to midnight. From midnight to sunrise the price was to be fixed by mutual agreement.

STEAMBOATS—Left from downtown New Orleans to fair-grounds. Schedule for various lines posted at steamship landings.
CURRENCY
Quartee—An imaginary 2½ cent piece
Picayune—5 cents
Nickel—5 cents
Two bits—25 cents
Four bits—50 cents
Six bits—75 cents
POSTAGE RATES IN THE UNITED STATES
First class mail—2 cents
Postcard—1 cent
ATTENDANCE
Anticipated—4,000,000
Actual—1,158,840
ENTERTAINMENT—daily parades, poetry readings, music of all kinds—from operas to march music, played by the master, John Philip Soussa; plays, "naval battles", army precision drill teams, cock fights, horse races, et cetera.
PERMANENT BUILDING—Horticultural Hall
Cost—$100,000
Construction—all wood and glass
Size—600 feet long by 194 feet wide with a 90-foot-tall glass tower in the center.
Fruit—20,000 plates on display at all times, doubling the number ever before displayed at any exposition.

To get people to visit their gardens the Japanese used an old New Orleans gimmick. They gave lagniappe in the form of seeds and instructed visitors to place them in waterways wherever they lived. Unfortunately, the seeds brought the water hyacinth to North America. The prolific "water lilies" have since caused un-ending problems in Southern waterways.

Played by Professor Pilcher, the organ installed in the Music Hall of the Main Building was the largest organ on the North American continent. The claim was made that the 32-foot brass pipes of the organ would generate enough volume to be heard for 4,000 miles *or less!* Professor Pilcher decided to extend the pipes to a point just beneath the ceiling, which would serve as a sounding board and spread the sound evenly throughout the building. Vibrations were so intense, however, that the ceiling boards began to flex and dance. Braces were pulled from their modest joints and Professor Pilcher and his magnificent organ *brought the roof down!* Fortunately no one was in the auditorium. The next day was April 1, 1885, but this was not an April Fool's joke. The *Daily Picayune* ran the full story which was picked up by a national newspaper wire service. Professor Pilcher now was able to claim that the sounds made by the mighty organ could be *read* about for *more* than 4,000 miles.

On February 11, 1885, exhibitors at the fair became so disenchanted with the management that 160 of them turned into an angry mob, broke down the exposition entrance gate and held an indignant meeting. A resolution suggesting that Congress be urged to defeat pending appropriations was threatened. Thanks to several leading exhibitors the threat was never carried out.

Two local newspapers sided with the mob. The *Daily Picayune* wrote that it did not wish to see the whole business community condemned because of the mismanagement of an enterprise over which it had no control. The *Mascot* newspaper said that the bubble had burst, Mardi Gras had come and gone, the days that were to redeem the great shows had passed and a colossal white elephant was floundering in a mire of stupidity, mismanagement and . . . corruption as helplessly as ever.

Apparently Major Burk was one of those men who worked at his best when the pressure was most intense. He was forever changing the plans in midstream and striving for a more grandiose facility. But the budget was suffering. With the deck stacked against him he packed his traveling bags and headed back to Washington, D.C. with his hand out. Eventually he persuaded Northern democrats, then committed completely to strict economy in federal spending, to grant a loan of a million dollars to the exposition plus a gift of $300,000 for the government exhibits. When the situation failed to improve he went back to Congress and convinced its members to appropriate another $350,000, not as a loan but as an outright gift to the fair. Major Burk was indeed persuasive.

The first electric streetcars in North America were installed at the 1884 fair. Two systems were tested to determine which was the most practical and trouble-free: an overhead power system and a third rail system whereby a rail in the ground supplied power. Proving to be the most efficient and trouble-free, the overhead system became the standard for all electric streetcars to follow. One of the world dignitaries to visit the 1884 fair was Sir Thomas Lipton of Lipton Tea fame, who became so engrossed with the new vehicle he stayed in New Orleans for several months to operate streetcars at every opportunity.

It was customary that Rex would arrive in New Orleans the day before Mardi Gras and be received at the St. Charles Hotel for a special dinner. In 1885 Rex showed his complete approval of the fair by making a trip by royal yacht to the fairgrounds. He was enthusiastically greeted and ushered onto the stage of the expansive Music Hall where he sat on a throne built especially in his honor.

The krewe showed its appreciation to the World's Fair by striking the first doubloon in the history of Mardi Gras. On one side of the doubloon was the coat of arms of the Rex organization. The other side had a picture of the main fair building. Thousands of the pewter medallions were given out on the next day.

As previously outlined, the fair was held primarily to celebrate the 100th anniversary of the exporting of cotton from North America to world markets and to give a boost to "The New South." The secondary reason as stated in the official visitor's guide to the fair was to give Negroes the first opportunity to show the world the progress they had achieved since their liberation from slavery.

But after the fair was over and had been evaluated the most important legacy became one that was not even considered before the fair. A Mrs. Howe of New Orleans, working in the women's department, presented an exhibit showing New Orleans' assorted memorabilia which had been shut up in the houses of Creole families. On display were jewels, laces, furniture, documents and a multitude of artifacts that had previously been taken for granted. Now the world was shown these remarkable items which had figured in the heritage of the people of New Orleans.

Grace King, a renowned writer, wrote of the most popular exhibit:

> "The exhibit's result was incredible, astounding, indeed it was the opening of the past history of the city not only to strangers but to the citizens themselves."

A large piece of iron ore currently located on the Audubon Park Golf Course was brought to the 1884 fair from Birmingham, Alabama. The legend that it is a meteorite is simply an old story handed down from generation to generation.

The only permanent structure built at the fair was the Horticultural Hall, but it was destroyed in the hurricane of 1915.

Since the grounds on which the fair was held was at one time the plantation of Louisiana's first historian, Charles Gayarré, a statue of the Goddess of History was installed on the fairgrounds. It is now located at the intersection of Esplanade Avenue, Tonti Street and Bayou Road. For some unknown reason it has been called for generations "The Mystery Monument," even though an inscription in the concrete walkway leading to it reads "Gayarré Place."

A second statue of another Louisiana historian, Alcée Fortier, was removed from the fairgrounds and has simply disappeared.

The ticket office for the street railway, built in the popular double-shotgun style of that time, still exists as an attractive uptown residence. Houses on Exposition Boulevard, built to house people working at the fair, still stand. Numerous other houses built for the fair were later sold at public auction, some put on barges and shipped upriver as far north as St. Louis.

The Mexican Pavillion was sold to the University of Alabama Medical School and taken to their Montezuma Medical College campus.

Fans that once cooled visitors to the 1884 World's Fair are still cooling patrons at Kolb's Restaurant, located in the 100 block of St. Charles Street.

Pipes from the powerful organ at the 1884 fair were purchased, installed and are still in use at Holy Name of Jesus Church on St. Charles Avenue across from Audubon Park, site of the 1884 fair.

The main gates of the '84 fair are now the main gates of the Jewish Cemetery on Elysian Fields Avenue.

Dozens of yards scattered throughout the city are today fenced with materials that surrounded the 1884 fair.

Exhibitors, guests, news media—almost all interested parties criticized the fair from the very beginning to the very end. The only area that escaped their wrath was New Orleans' food; in fact, restaurants were the subject of a great deal of bubbling commentary. One newspaper account described the commodious restaurants and lunch stands as "establishments managed by experts where the inner man can be quickly served with good food at prices that are really moderate."

Lafcadio Hearn, a nationally-known writer who worked in New Orleans for several years, recognized the brilliance of the local cuisine and rushed into print a book entitled, "La Cuisine Creole" that was written especially to be sold at the fair.

Most visiting journalists wrote more about how different and interesting New Orleans was and about the cuisine rather than about the Exposition and the New South.

No matter how good the taste of the food, the bitter taste of financial problems was always dished up to Major Burk. On May 13, with poor press, bad weather and deplorable attendance that was only half of the projected number, he resigned his position stating that demands of his business were too great for him to carry on this wonderful project.

On its bumbling course the exposition continued until June 1, 1885, when it was officially scheduled to come to an end. But even the closing ceremony was controversial. Since June 1 fell on a Sunday there were those who adamantly opposed anything of this nature taking place on the Sabbath. Therefore, the ceremony was put off until June 2, 1885. The ceremony was brief and about as entertaining as a wake.

In order to minimize some of the financial losses the buildings and grounds were used for the North Central and South American Exposition, which ran from November 10, 1885 to March 31, 1886, with about the same results as the 1884 fair.

Buildings on the grounds were finally sold at public auction to a dealer in second-hand materials. While the Government Building cost $750,000 to build, it sold for $4,100. The Main Building cost $1,000,000 and sold for $9,050.

Major E. A. Burk ran into a little problem a short time after the fair. He was still the state's treasurer and an audit of his department revealed a shortage of $1,777,000. Indicted for embezzlement and forgery, he fled to London, England.

From London he denounced the charges and promised an

early return to clear his name. Instead, knowing what was awaiting his return to Louisiana, he went to Honduras and was for many years a fugitive from Louisiana courts. He then began a crusade in Honduras to redeem the country from its backward conditions.

Knowing the tenacity and drive of Major Burk, we can only surmise that he became a driving force in the affairs of Honduras. After all, he allegedly had $1,777,000 of Louisiana's money with which to work.

Longtime New Orleanian Sidney Bowman went to the 1928 and 1932 Olympics as a hop-step jumper.

CHAPTER TEN

Sports

Since the founding of our city its people have participated in and excelled in almost every sport played in North America. Moreover, they have excelled in some not played anywhere else on the face of the earth. Example: New Orleanians play softball by fast pitching overhand and use standard baseball measurements between the bases.

We have a very short winter season in New Orleans; in 1983 it was on a *Wednesday afternoon*. Couple this with the fact that the two highest spots of land in New Orleans are a 28½-foot hill built in 1937 by the W.P.A. in Audubon Park (called Monkey Hill) and a 42-foot hill (unnamed) made from earth removed for I-610. One can readily understand why our people have not excelled in winter sports.

The second area in which we have not yet excelled is professional football. Although our New Orleans Saints were organized in 1966 they have not yet had a winning season. On the opening kickoff of the first league game against the Los Angeles Rams, Saints player John Gilliam ran the ball back for a touchdown thus scoring points in the first ten seconds of official league play for a record that will probably stand for a long time. But grand debuts do not a game or season or seasons make.

Some disgruntled season-ticket holders who have been faithful since 1966 say the Saints problems are twofold:

1. They use the same scouts recruited by General Custer.
2. The opposing defensive team always knows which Saint will carry the football. Looking into the backfield, they spot the one with tears of fear in his eyes.

BOXING

As a rough and tumble port city filled with men who loved to fight and had the strength, stamina, and agility to do it well, New Orleans has had more than its share of world champions.

Although New Orleanians have been fighting since the inception of the city, the first official prize fight, according to the *National Fleischers Ring Record Book*, was held in New Orleans on May 6, 1836, between two powerful New Orleans Irishmen named James Burk and Sam O'Rourke.

The first legal boxing match ever held in the United States was held in New Orleans in 1890. Boxing gloves were first used in an 1891 boxing match in New Orleans between Louis Nuckols and Charles Carroll. The longest recorded fight ever held was endured in New Orleans on April 6, 1893, between Jack Burk and Andy Bower; it lasted 110 rounds over a period of seven hours and 19 minutes and ended in a draw.

Neither man received a dime for his efforts. Rules of the day called for the winner to receive the entire purse. Since this fight ended in a draw both men received cuts, bruises and battered bodies. Nothing else.

New Orleans is the only city to ever have three world championship fights on three consecutive days:

1. September 5, 1892, lightweight championship.
   Jack McAuliffe knocked out Billy Meyers with $9,000 to the winner.
2. September 6, featherweight championship.
   George Dixon knocked out Jack Skelly. Winner received $7,500.
3. September 7, heavyweight championship.
   A 34-year-old Jack Dempsey was knocked out by 26-year-old Gentleman James J. Corbett; the winner received $25,000 tax-free.

Fight fans of New Orleans in the 1850s were so volatile that barbed wire had to be strung around the ring to protect the judges, referee and fighters. That's taking a sport seriously!

ODDS AND ENDS

Although New Orleans has never had a major league baseball team, over the years the city has supplied more than its share of outstanding players and managers to America's No. 1 sport. (In Louisiana it's No. 2. Since the first election in New Orleans in 1812, politics have been and remain the leading sport.)

Abner Powell, who was the inventor of ladies day in baseball, turned the spectator sport from *men only* into a family sport that immediately transformed the game into our national pastime. Because of New Orleans' unrelenting rainfall, Abner also popularized the raincheck and the infield cover.

New Orleans has the oldest tennis (1874) and chess clubs in the United States, the second-oldest yacht club (1849) and the third-oldest horse-racing track (1872).

In 1902 the Fair Grounds had a well-known figure as its betting commissioner. Frank James, brother of the notorious Jesse James, was pardoned by the governor of Missouri to assume his new duties. Frank's knowledge of racing was extensive, and the Fair Grounds needed his services. Before the Civil War New Orleans had the top track in the country: the Metairie Race Course which is now the Metairie Cemetery.

The first superstars of sports in North America were the fencing masters of Exchange Place in the French Quarter. In their day they received the same adulation as the Joe Namaths, Mickey Mantles, Wilt Chamberlains and Hank Aarons of today. New Orleans had the first North American world champion of chess, Paul Morphy, and now is the home of the largest sporting arena in the World, the Louisiana Superdome. Attendance records are constantly being set in this phenomenal arena, which is truly one of the man-made wonders of the world.

THE FIRST TEAM SPORT
PLAYED IN NEW ORLEANS

The first team sport played in the New Orleans area was a

Choctaw Indian game closely resembling lacrosse called stick ball or raquette. To work off hostility Indians played this game. The original site of the Indian game was on the plains of Gentilly. Each team was allowed to have 80 players on the field; no substitutes were allowed. Shoeless and stripped to the waist, team members distinguished one side from the other by wearing different colors of paint. The field was 600 yards long and 300 yards wide with a pole erected in the center called a *bomboula*.

A leather ball slightly larger than a tennis ball was thrown in the center of the field as the game began. Each player carried two raquettes (hence the French name "raquette"): a short one for scooping the ball from the ground and a long one for throwing the ball at the target. Often both sticks were used to strike opponents without mercy.

A target made of animal skins was posted on top of tall frames at each end of the field. When the ball hit the target the scoring team received a *pelotte*, or point.

Lasting for several days, the fast and fierce game was officiated by six officials: two to keep score and three to keep time (one representing each team and one impartial). The sixth official simply threw the ball out on the field to start the game and retrieved it when it went out of bounds.

Bloody noses, knocked out teeth, broken legs and other miscellaneous fractures were not unusual; raquette definitely was not a sissy's game. When the game was over, victorious team members carried their captain around the field on their shoulders, sang a victory song and whooped up with the tribe's cry.

The game was adopted and played by black slaves and later by the Creoles of New Orleans.

By the year 1900 the game that had been so popular had vanished completely from the New Orleans sporting scene. In some parts of South Louisiana, Indians still play updated versions of this ancient contest.

UNUSUAL SPORTS OF THE PAST

Compared to the sports of the 1800s, pro-football would have to be considered tame. Many of the earliest "games" pitted animal against animal.

The first world champion from the United States was New Orleans Creole Paul Morphy, who became world chess champion in 1858. In this scene in England, Morphy plays blind against eight players simultaneously. (The Historic New Orleans Collection)

Cock fights, which by the way are today illegal but still around, were extremely popular with the Creoles. As many as 20 cocks were placed in a ring and the last one standing was declared the winner. If a cock was groggy after a few rounds its owner was permitted to revive him during the rest period by crushing garlic toes into a jigger of bourbon, drawing the mixture into a straw-like cylinder and blowing it down the rooster's nostrils. After that treatment the cock was supercharged and ready to fight to the death.

One "class act" featured a dog called "the green machine." His master would wager that his canine would kill 50 rats in 60 seconds; he never lost a bet.

Promoters were always devising means of extracting money from their customers. On September 5, 1817, the *Courier* newspaper ran the following list of sporting events scheduled for the neutral ground on Canal Street: An Attakapas bull versus six of the strongest dogs in America, six bulldogs against a Canadian bear, a tiger against a black bear, 12 dogs opposing an Appaloosa bull. There was a fifth fight scheduled if the tiger survived his first encounter. Unfortunately for the paying customers and the tiger, it did not.

By 1823, the practice of pitting animals against animals had degenerated to the point that the *Louisiana Gazette* ran the following article:

> Over and over again we have heard New Orleans reproached with the manner in which the Sabbath Evening is kept by many of the inhabitants, but never was a more brutal pastime than that in Canal Street yesterday afternoon.
>
> In sight and hearing of the two churches during the time of the afternoon services, some 150 individuals in the garb of gentlemen and at least 50 well-dressed females patiently sit and see a poor bull worried by a score of dogs in a narrow pen. If such cruel sports are continued, the City Hall will merit the taint of being a reproach to the Union.

NEW ORLEANS' FIRST FOOTBALL GAME

College football today bears no resemblance to the first Princeton vs. Rutgers game of November 6, 1869. With 25 men on

each side the game began with a kick of the ball to the quarterback
(hence the name football). A combination more like soccer and prize
fighting, pushing and shoving resulted in plays lasting up to five
minutes.

On January 1, 1890, at Sportsman Park New Orleanians witnessed their first football game, held on that date because college
students were home for the holidays from schools in the East. A

The first football game played in New Orleans took place on January 1, 1890. The
contest ended abruptly after a booming kick sent the city's only football into the
New Basin Canal. (Drawing by Laine Casteix)

benefit game, one team represented Princeton and the other side Yale. Adding color to the game, the referee wore a tall silk hat.

Following is the flourishing description of the game in the January 2, 1890, *Picayune:*

> Yesterday, fairness nowhere appeared to better advantage than upon the broad green field at Sportsman Park with sturdy, pictur-esque oaks at the far end and the grandstand filled with the choicest flowers of New Orleans' society.
>
> The game lasted less than 45 minutes with a score of 0 to 0. The game ended abruptly because of an over-enthusiastic kick that sent the city's only football spinning into the New Basin Canal, where with a ruptured bladder it slowly sank out of sight.

THE FIRST TULANE—L.S.U. GAME

The advent of football in New Orleans came through the concerted efforts of a Tulane professor named T. L. Bayne, a for-mer star quarterback for Yale University and Captain of the South-ern Athletic Club. He was instrumental in scheduling a game in 1893 between Tulane and his club. Not one to leave the work to others, this one-man gang took on the following responsibilities:

—He was appointed coach of the Tulane team.
—Bayne selected the school colors of olive and blue.
—He secured one of the few footballs in Louisiana.
—The prof-coach marked the field, erected goal posts, printed tick-ets, sold them door to door, and came up with the Tulane yell:
  Rah, Rah, Rah
      Sis boom bah
      Rah, Rah, Rah, Tulane.

Finally, he officiated the game on November 18, 1893, which was won by Southern Athletic Club in the relative privacy of Sportsman Park.

Lack of interest on the part of the fans did not dampen Bayne's enthusiasm for the gridiron. He contacted Dr. Charles E. Coates, LSU Chemistry professor, to schedule a game for the following weekend. Since LSU had just organized its team, Bayne had to assist the coach, Dr. Coates, in getting his men ready to play their first game.

The match between the two universities became big box office. Tickets (at 50 cents each) sold like hotcakes both in Baton Rouge and New Orleans.

On the morning of the game, LSU quarterback Ruffin Pleasant, Coach Coates and a few players went to town to buy ribbon to brighten up the initial contest. S. I. Reymond's store had in stock a large supply of purple and gold ribbon for the approaching Mardi Gras season, but the green had not yet arrived. Badges and rosettes were made of the available material and colors for the all-male student body, numbering 200, which along with President James W. Nicholson, followed the LSU team to New Orleans.

Winning the first game was apparently very important to both teams. Tulane made no secret of the fact that it had picked up several Southern Athletic Club players and LSU had a "ringer" in the person of LSU professor Harcourt A. Morgan, who had played during his college days.

Although there was a sizable contingent of fans in the stands on that cold and cloudy day of November 25, 1893, a continuous flow of carriages heading out Canal Street toward New Basin and Sportsman Park was creating a traffic jam.

At game time 2,000 fans witnessed the tossing of two coins, one for the choice of goal and one for possession. Players were warned not to pay any attention to train whistles.

LSU won the toss for choice of goal but little else. Tulane won possession of the ball and ultimately the game by a score of 34 to 0. Tulane scored a total of seven touchdowns and three conversions. Scoring in those days was quite different from what it is today. Field goals and touchdowns were good for four points each; conversions and safeties, two points.

In this highly-publicized and well-attended first Louisiana college football game only one player weighed over 200 pounds. His name was Walter Castenado and he weighed in at 220. Some players were as light as 135 pounds and members of both teams averaged 155 pounds per man.

Interesting highlights included a goal-line stand with LSU holding Tulane for four downs on the four-yard line. Tulane's 135-

pound end, Robelot, was knocked senseless and removed from the game. Hugh Bayne, an exceptional Tulane player, left the game at half time. A carriage was waiting to take him to a law lecture.

LSU's Captain Pleasant was injured seriously during the first half and carried from the field by his teammates. Later he would be carried again by his supporters to election as governor of Louisiana.

LSU's 155-pound right halfback, Edwin F. Gayle, was in the game for every play. His durability in football could have been a prognostication of his durability in the game of life. A Lake Charles attorney later, he lived well past 100 years of age.

After the first Louisiana collegiate game, LSU players and fans boarded the special train (the first train ever used to transport a student body to a football game) for the trip back to Baton Rouge.

Exuberant Tulane fans congregated in downtown New Orleans to savor the victory. They marched down Camp Street to the newspaper office where they repeatedly yelled their Tulane cheer and the final score (34-0) to insure a story in the paper on the next day.

While LSU's official colors in 1893 were blue and white, the colors (purple and gold) of the Mardi Gras materials available for that first game were adopted instead and have been used ever since. It is interesting to note that the two major universities in Louisiana, LSU and Tulane, together have the three Mardi Gras colors as their school colors: purple and gold . . . and green.

NEW ORLEANS' FIRST
PROFESSIONAL FOOTBALL GAME

The first professional football game in New Orleans was held on January 10, 1926, at Heinemann Park between the world champion Chicago Bears and the Southern All-Stars from Tulane, Lafayette, Central, Auburn, Vanderbilt and LSU.

Although there were some great pros and all-stars playing in this game no one doubted the fact that most people came out to see Red Grange, the "galloping ghost," who did not disappoint his fans. He carried the ball 16 times, averaged four-and-a-half yards per carry, scored one touchdown and returned a punt for 51 yards (it was called back due to clipping). In the third quarter Red broke through the line and was headed for another touchdown but was tackled on the four-yard line by Tulane's Lester Lautenschlaeger. The All-Stars not only held, but they threw the world champions back for two losses.

The All-Stars had their own heroes, including a runner named Brown who broke loose for a 36-yard gain which outshined Red's longest run. Defensively Tulane's left guard, Gene Hergeret, was sensational, so much so that the "galloping ghost" played for over three quarters of the game—something unheard of for Red.

All-Star quarterback Lautenschlaeger improved as the game continued. He ran the team well, intercepted a pass, and stripped off several good runs himself. In the fourth quarter he unleashed a passing attack that had the Bears worried. But time was running out and when the final whistle blew the world champion Chicago Bears had beaten the Southern All-Stars 14-0.

The All-Stars had nothing to be ashamed of. They had held the world champions to nine first downs and had forced Number 77 to play almost all of the game.

AUTO VERSUS AIRPLANE

In the early 1900s, we see the introduction of both the automobile and the airplane to New Orleans. Although air travel was available in our city as early as the 1850s in the form of hot air balloons it was not until 1910 that winged flight made its debut on the scene.

It is not known when the first automobile reached our city, but a world auto record was set in New Orleans in 1909 when Rolph dePalma exceeded 60 miles per hour on the New Basin Canal shell road, an event that helped to popularize the horseless carriage.

In 1911 Louisiana initiated the construction of highways and by 1912 automobiles were so popular in New Orleans that on April 14, 1912, the *Picayune* advertised the latest innovation: Goodyear Tire and Rubber Company, located at 536 Baronne Street, offered *free* air for auto tires.

Shortly after Rolph dePalma's world auto speed record New Orleans hosted its first international aviation tournament. One of the planes at the tournament rose to over 7,000 feet and recorded a mile in 57 seconds. Someone thought it would be interesting to

On December 30, 1910, pioneer aviator John B. Moisant raced a Packard automobile and lost by a whisker. (Drawing by Laine Casteix)

pit the automobile against the airplane; the result was the featured event of the International Aviation Tournament held at City Park on December 30, 1910.

The competing automobile was a 150-horsepower Packard driven by Joe Seymour. The airplane, a Bleriot with a 50-horsepower engine, was piloted by John B. Moisant.

Jut about everyone thought the airplane would complete the five-mile course around the horse track ahead of the car. But while the airplane outdistanced its rival in the straight stretch, the Packard made up for less speed in the turns and beat John B. Moisant's airplane by a whisker.

On the very next day, December 31, 1910, Moisant was attempting to break a speed record. Upon leaving City Park air strip he headed for Harahan, Louisiana, where he was to begin his record attempt. Hitting an air pocket, he was thrown from the airplane (there were no seat belts then) and was killed instantly, becoming the 30th fatality among pioneer airmen in the world.

Since the site on which he lost his life is in the approximate vicinity of what we now call New Orleans International Airport, the field to this day carries his name: Moisant.

You're truly an Orleanian when you enjoy a speech by Jimmy Fitzmorris *(top)*, support a benefit by Joe Gimelli *(above left)* and believe a weather report by Nash Roberts *(above right)*. (Photos courtesy of subjects)

CHAPTER ELEVEN

*Y*ou're Truly *An Orleanian When . . .*

You're truly an Orleanian when . . .

1. You know that "C.D.M." on the coffee can stands for Cafe du Monde.

2. Someone *ax* you to cross the *neutral ground* to get three *alligator pears,* two *mirlitons* and *lagniappe* from the vendor on the *banquette* and you know exactly what he or she means.

3. Schools let out, all work stops, traffic becomes snarled and everyone congregates outdoors to watch a dozen or so snowflakes fall, knowing well that replays of this phenomenon will be shown on every local TV station for the next two weeks.

4. Every evening during carnival you rush to get to a parade and arrive two hours early so that you can sit in the gutter and have a three-course meal consisting of peanuts, cotton candy and apples-on-the stick, and you consider this normal behavior.

5. Attempting to cross the Greater New Orleans Bridge at peak hours you have time to visit friends, buy coffee, doughnuts and chewing gum from vendors thereon. And you look upon this as a typical trip on the most patriotic bridge in the world, "the car strangled spanner."

6. You've heard Jimmy Fitzmorris give a talk, have attended a charity function headed by Joe Gimelli, and have kept up with the weather with Nash Roberts.

7. You get a good laugh when commercials produced by national companies refer to Met-tear-ree (Metairie).

8. You slow-drip coffee and chicory a few spoonfuls at a time so that a spoon can stand up in it.

9. *You* can cross the neutral ground on Canal Street but perpendicular streets do not.

10. You drink burgundy wine but pronounce the street "ber-gun-dee."

11. You stomp fiercely on anything that hits the ground and makes a clanging sound like a doubloon.

12. You know the city has two kinds of "ferries" and have learned to appreciate one and accept the other.

13. Standing on Canal Street and facing the river you can look up to see the ships passing.

14. You can't remember not seeing roaches in your home on two consecutive days.

15. You drive your car for three blocks, hit only eight holes and get out to see if you missed one.

16. You blink twice a year and miss autumn and spring.

17. You expect the meteorologists to give the same summer weather forecast for 90 straight days.

18. You get out of an elevator on a humid day stuck to the guy next to you and you don't think there's anything unusual about the cohesion.

19. You give directions when asked where Monkey Hill is located.

20. You see a parade followed by people shaking, gyrating, twisting and turning and you know they are not spasmodic but merely second-lining.

21. Your definition of a seven-course meal is a six-pack of Dixie beer and a poorboy.

22. You know the correct way to cook red beans is upside down so that they only give you hiccups.

23. You go to a St. Patrick's Day parade to get the makings for dinner knowing that cabbage, potatoes and green bananas will be thrown from floats.

24. A friend tells you to meet him at the walled ovens in the nearest cemetery and you know what he means.

25. Someone asks if you suck the heads and eat the tails and you reply, "Of course, doesn't everyone?" (of crawfish, of course).

You're truly an Orleanian when you understand that sucking heads and eating tails has to do with crawfish. (Louisiana Tourist Commission, photo by Noel Blakely)

26. You know Rex means King, so you don't say King of Rex.

27. You have 190 pounds of seafood but only 10 pounds of meat in your freezer.

28. You not only listen to Dixie to soothe your nerves but you drink it as well to quench your thirst.

29. You call Barq's, "root beer," even though the company spends loads of money telling you it's not.

30. On a summer morning, with the sun shining brightly and no clouds in the sky, you take an umbrella when you leave for work.

31. You hear clanging sounds and you think of a streetcar or the Roman candy man rather than a fire engine.

32. You know the fleur-de-lis is the emblem of the New Orleans Saints and also has something to do with France but you're not sure what.

33. You know the first Superdome in New Orleans was Pete Fountain's head.

34. You know a hooker is not the name of a Confederate General.

35. You know better than to inhale when eating beignets with powdered sugar.

36. You have heard about the meteorite that fell in Audubon Park (even though it's not a meteorite at all).

37. You know the YMCA is located across from the statue of Robert E. Lee as a reminder to him that the Yankees Might Come Again.

38. You listen to a political speech and believe it.

39. You know that politics is now and always has been the leading sport in the Crescent City.

40. You know that an Old Regular had nothing to do with daily constitutions but concerns a member of a political party.

41. You listen to Buddy deLiberto on television and understand every word he says.

42. You listen to Black Cat Lacombe give his Fairgrounds handicap and then bet on any other horse.

43. You know Smokey Mary wasn't a heavy smoker but the old train that ran on Elysian Fields Avenue from the river to the lake.

44. You're as confused about the original meaning of the word Creole as other Orleanians and visitors.

45. The term shotgun house does not bring a frown to your forehead.

46. The points on a New Orleans compass are not North, South, East and West, but Uptown, Downtown, River and Lake.

47. You put plastic Mardi Gras beads into the oven to make knickknacks.

48. You tell visitors New Orleans is the only major city in America without a street named "Main."

49. You leave home six hours early to get to Moisant Airport for a Friday afternoon flight.

50. You know that shrimp doesn't mean small.

51. You stand in line for more than an hour to buy a Hansen's snowball.

52. You listen to Dr. Frank Minyard play his trumpet and you think you're listening to music.

53. You can name without hesitation the number of New Orleans Saints coaches who have had winning seasons.

54. You drink New Orleans water and forget about the chemical, petro-chemical and other industrial plants located upstream.

55. You read about an alligator getting into someone's swimming pool in New Orleans East and simply mutter, "What, again?"

56. You read the *Times-Picayune* and the *States Item* and assume you're getting independent views.

57. You go into a cemetery and know you'd better have a flak jacket or police escort or both.

58. You attend a wake and expect to hear the latest jokes.

59. You watch Channel 12 and wonder what's wrong if you don't witness a fund-raising pitch during the evening.

60. You know the proper sequence of religious upbringing in Catholic faith is: (1) To be christened. (2) To make your first Communion. (3) To be confirmed. (4) To play bingo weekly.

61. You don't necessarily expect rain when the humidity reaches 100 percent.

62. You recognize a poorboy not as an underachiever but as

an overachiever, especially if served sloppy and dressed all the way.

63. You admit there are better places in the world but you concede you can't have them moved here.

64. You know Orleans Parish is the smallest parish in the state landwise, yet it has the largest population of any of the 64 parishes in the state and that the Louisiana Superdome has 64 sky boxes named for each of the parishes.

65. You have at least three Schwegmann Giant Supermarket bags in your home.

66. You read Hap Glaudi's column in the newspaper, watch him on television, or listen to him on his radio broadcast and believe what he says.

67. You have spent, cumulatively, at least a week over the past 25 years parked in traffic on the Greater New Orleans Bridge.

68. You know why New Orleans is called the Crescent City.

69. You know the Vieux Carré is the land of Queens and in-betweens.

70. You hear a Wayne Mack interview, and you feel better that he, too, is truly an Orleanian.

71. Someone asks, "Where y'at?" and the term has nothing whatsoever to do with physical location.

CHAPTER TWELVE

New Orleans Terminology

ARMOIRE: A decorative wooden wardrobe for holding clothes. Early laws taxed every room in a house and since closets were considered rooms, taxes were lessened by using an armoire in place of a locker.

Since hallways were also considered rooms the same tax-saving reasoning brought about the use of outside stairways and galleries, especially galleries on the sides of houses. Gallery undersides were often painted sky blue with paint fortified with liquid camphor. It was believed that the blue color would confuse insects into thinking they were looking up at the sky. Distasteful to most insects, the camphor aroma was further deterrence to the critters.

ARPENT: Old French measure of land which varied in value with the locality. In Louisiana and French Canada (the only regions in North America where the measure was used) an arpent was 180 French feet. Just as a French heel is more than an ordinary heel, so is a French foot more than the ordinary foot; 100 French feet are equivalent to 106¼ feet.

BANQUETTE: A sidewalk—the word meaning a low bench, like a church kneeler (see Chapter V, page 74 for explanation).

BAYOU: Taken from the Indian word *boyuks*, a stream which flows from a river or lake into another body of water; a natural

Briquette Entre Poteaux simply means brick between posts. (Louisiana Tourist Commission)

spillway. In the days before roads, bayous were considered the secondary means of travel and the rivers were primary.

BITS: A monetary designation. The Mexican trade dollar, used extensively in early New Orleans, was broken into eight basic parts. Each "bit" was worth 12½ cents; two bits, 25 cents. When there were shortages of the small bit coins the round Mexican dollar was cut into pieces, or bits. Two bits placed point to point resembled a bitte or "bitt-head" on which English sailors made fast their hawsers.

Half of a *picayune* was a *cuartillo* but it became known in New Orleans as the *quartee*. When a mother sent a child to the grocery store to buy beans and rice, the child was reminded to ask for "a quartee of beans and a quartee of rice and little bit of pickled meat as lagniappe to make it all taste nice."

In counting the Mexican trade dollar, bankers would draw half of an eight, symbolizing the Spanish dollar, and then drew a line through it for each dollar counted; hence, the origin of the dollar sign ($).

BRIQUETTE ENTRE POTEAUX: (French for brick between posts.) An eighteenth-century method of construction in which bricks were inserted between spaces in a framework of cypress timbers. (Excellent example: Lafitte's Blacksmith Shop located at 941 Bourbon Street.)

CAJUN: The corruption of the word "Acadian."

In the middle of the 1700s France lost another of its long-running wars with England. Those French people who were living in Acadia, Canada (now called Nova Scotia, meaning New Scotland) and refused to pledge allegiance to the crown were herded aboard ships to be deposited along the eastern seaboard. Over a period of 30 years approximately 4,000 of them migrated to Louisiana where they were welcomed by the French Creoles who were living under Spanish control at the time. (The King of France could no longer support Louisiana and had given it to his cousin, Charles III of Spain, to keep the English from taking it.)

Cajuns are people who live life to the fullest, who love to dance, sing and tell jokes, even on themselves. They eat boudin (blood sausage), hog cracklins, gumbo, crawfish, sauce piquante; in fact, some say they will eat anything that does not eat them first. As hard-working as they are fun-loving, they accept people for what they are not what others think of them. They accept strangers with open arms but injustice will turn a Cajun into an alligator with two heads.

CAFÉ AU LAIT: Boiled milk and coffee mixed in equal proportions and used as a breakfast drink.

CAFÉ NOIR: Black coffee—early morning and after-dinner drink.

COFFEE AND CHICORY: (See Chapter I, page 15).

COFFEE BRÛLOT: A spiced coffee flamed with brandy and served after dinner.

SLOW-DRIP COFFEE: Since Creoles liked their coffee strong they used the slow drip method in making their favorite drink.

About two tablespoons of boiling water were poured over the grounds. When the puffing and bubbling ceased more water was poured. Too much water at the beginning of the process resulted in weaker coffee because the grounds were not yet ready to release their strength. Once the grounds settled down the slow-pouring process proceeded until the desired amount of coffee was brewed.

CREOLE: A white descendant of the French and Spanish settlers in Louisiana.

The word came from the Spanish word *criollo,* believed by the proud Spanish people to mean "from the thigh of Jupiter." The word "Creole" was not used in the City of New Orleans until the year 1765 when the Spanish took control of Louisiana. It did not take the French long to realize the word was a positive term; they adopted it and changed its spelling to the present "Creole."

How did the word Creole come to be misused? French Creole plantation owners sent their slaves into town to sell crops, instructing slaves to advise the people that these were Creole products, and therefore, far superior to any others available. They were extremely successful in selling the fruits and vegetables raised by the Creoles. Thus, we came to have Creole tomatoes, Creole corn, Creole mules and Creole blacks. It was only logical that since they, the slaves, were also owned by the Creoles, they considered themselves to be Creole slaves.

In spite of being used for 200 years, Creole is still one of the most misunderstood words in New Orleans and out. It would be safe to say that most visitors to the city think Creole denotes a person with white and black blood.

A good explanation of the present-day use of the word Creole is brought out explicity in the book *Gumbo Yaya* by Lyle Saxon, Edward Dreyer and Robert Tallant. The authors emphatically state that no true Creole ever had Negro blood. There are proud, light-colored people in New Orleans today who are known as Creoles among themselves, but Creoles were always white. Any trace of *café au lait* in the negro family was reason for complete ostracism. A few years back a very fine Creole cook named Leon Soniat did a series of television shows on Creole cooking for a national network. Upon receiving the tapes the network realized he was a white man and refused the series under the title of Creole cooking because it was felt that, nationally-speaking, people think of Creoles as being black people. It is easy to understand why others would like to be considered Creoles "from the thigh of Jupiter," crème de la crème, pièce de résistance. Who would not like to be counted in that number?

DIXIE: The southern states of the United States.

The term came about because of a $10.00 bill circulated before the Civil War. Keelboatmen from upriver, upon reaching New Orleans and selling their cargo, were ready and anxious to spend their money. The downtown shopping area was unique at that time. On one side of Canal Street French money was used and on the other side American money was the currency. When the keelboatmen complained about the inconvenience the Citizens Bank on Toulouse Street printed a $10.00 bill with both English and French designations for ten. Since *dix* is ten in French, keelboatmen corrupted the word in saying, "We're going to New Orleans to get some of those good old Dixies."

In 1859 the song "Dixie" was written by the black minstrel actor Daniel D. Emmett. It was played for the first time in New York City with very little acceptance. Not until after John Owen, manager of the Variety Theater in New Orleans on Gravier Street, used it as a marching song for 40 female Zouaves did the song fuel the spirit of southern nationalism. Ever since, it has been popular with our people as the Confederate national anthem.

GALLERY: Balcony on a Creole house.

GARÇONNIERE: Bachelor quarters or guest room in the wing at the rear of the main house or in the attic, often above the front porch.

HUSH PUPPIES: An Indian fried-meal cake. Spreading through the South the creation supposedly received its name in

Shotgun house derives its name from the saying that one can open the front and back doors and shoot a shotgun through the house without hitting anything. (Louisiana Tourist Commission)

Georgia when someone fed some to a pack of howling hunting dogs with the admonition: Hush Puppies!

So, just as jazz was born in New Orleans and received its name in Chicago, the hush puppy is another New Orleans creation that received it's name in another state.

SHOTGUN HOUSE: A very narrow, long house with doors at the front and the rear.

The shotgun house came into existence when large numbers of poor Irish immigrants arrived in the city with nowhere to live. The riverfront was lined for miles with flatboats with their cargoes protected by narrow sheds. Because there was no power yet to go back upriver, the storage structures on the barges were taken off the boats and deposited on the land near the Irish section where they were soon adopted as homes. It was said that a shotgun could be fired from the front door entrance to the back door of the long, narrow houses without hitting anything.

SHOTGUN DOUBLE: The same as above, except two narrow, long houses were put together for larger Irish families.

CAMEL-BACK HOUSE: Because taxes were assessed according to the number of rooms as well as the number of openings in the front of the house, additions were made on the back of res-

A camelback house has a single story in front and two in the rear, a design aiming to avoid local taxes that were levied according to the number of openings (windows and doors) in the front of a home. (Photo from Buddy Stall Collection)

idences to avoid additional assessment on the domiciles.

JAMBALAYA: A Spanish Creole dish made with rice and seafood or meat.

JAZZ FUNERAL: A funeral for a prominent citizen usually associated with music. Slow jazz is played on the way to the funeral, and hot, fast jazz is played once the body has been entombed.

In the twentieth century jazz funerals are a "take off" on nineteenth century Irish musical funerals that usually were accompanied by a brass band.

Funeral parades with jazz bands have customarily been followed by what has been termed a "second line." The second line is made up of people who are not an official part of the parade but who join in spontaneously to show their enthusiasm for the music. A decorated umbrella has become a traditional part of second-lining, which is also common at parades other than jazz funerals.

KING CAKE: (See Chapter I, page 7).

LAGNIAPPE: A little something extra given with a purchase. A premium.

This tradition is still observed in New Orleans culture and dates back to Normandy, France and Acadia, Canada. When driven out by the British the Acadians brought to New Orleans this generous practice. In selling grain to customers it was placed in a woolen cloth, known in France as *nappe*. To compensate the buyer for grain caught in the nappe the seller would throw in a couple of handfuls from his supply without charge saying, "C'est pour là nappe," meaning that which was caught in the cloth.

By giving this extra service to the purchaser a satisfied and repeat customer was often assured. Lagniappe is a word that is heard frequently in New Orleans. A number of business people still give it to their good customers.

LOCKER: Equivalent to a closet.

MAKING GROCERIES: Shopping at a supermarket for food items.

MARDI GRAS: "Shrove Tuesday" or "Fat Tuesday," the day before Lent begins during which time Christians fatten up and celebrate in preparation for the denials of penance and fasting during the ensuing 40 days of Lent.

NAPOLEONIC CODE: Louisiana is the only state in the Union that operates under the Napoleonic code of laws, borrowing from the common law of England and the civil law of Rome. The common law of England professes that the power of government must never overshadow the rights of man. The civil law of Rome, modified by the noblest thoughts of France and Spain, maintains that the lasting foundation for right and justice is to be found in the Golden Rule.

MUFFULETTA: (See Chapter I, page 14).

NEUTRAL GROUND: (See Chapter III, page 51).

PARISH: Louisiana word for county.

Again, Louisiana is the only state with civil subdivisions of parishes rather than counties. Under both France and Spain from 1682 to 1893 Louisiana was governed by Catholic nations with no separation between church and state. It was customary to build the government around the church and vice versa. Thus, the church parish was the political subdivision as well. When the territory was sold to the United States it was divided into two sections: the territory of Louisiana and the territory of Orleans. Together the two territories approximated Louisiana as it is today, with the addition of eight other parishes north of Lake Pontchartrain which still belonged to Spain.

PICAYUNE: Originally a small Spanish coin valued at six-and-a-quarter cents.

PIROGUE: A small, canoe-like boat.

Indians made this type of boat by hollowing out a log. They used this mode of transportation for over 1,000 years before the coming of the white man. Designed with a slender tip on each end, this maneuverable craft could go in either direction. Bottoms were flat to permit easy portage across land. A larger unit could hold up to 12 tons.

The Spaniards are said to have brought the name *piraga* (dugout) from the Caribbean to Canada and it found its way from there to Louisiana. Reference to pirogues in Louisiana date back as early as 1718 when Antoine LePage DuPratz made note of the Indians' use of pirogues to great advantage in marshes, bayous and rivers. The pirogue was to early Louisiana what the covered wagon was to the West. Although the covered wagon has now disappeared it is doubtful that the pirogue, because of its functional attributes, will ever completely disappear from our state.

PISTOLETTE: (See Chapter I, page 7).

POINTS ON THE COMPASS IN NEW ORLEANS: Not North, South, East, West but Uptown, Downtown, River, Lake.

Located in the crescent of the river with streets curving and turning it is not easy to give directions of North, South, East and West. However, using Canal Street as the axis, everything upriver from the axis is uptown, everything downriver from the axis is classified downtown, while the axis points toward the river or toward the lake.

Everything across the river from New Orleans is called the West Bank, which in itself is confusing to outsiders. To get to Algiers from New Orleans you travel east to get to the West Bank. Although confusing to others, New Orleanians assume this is the way it is done everywhere.

With South Claiborne and South Carrollton crossing, it is easy to understand why New Orleanians use the terms Uptown, Downtown, River and Lake to give directions instead of North, South, East and West. (Photo by Noel Blakely)

POKER: While the game of craps (dice) was brought to New Orleans by millionaire playboy Bernard Marigny, the game of poker started here. A combination of a French game called *poque*, the Parisian game of "As Nas" and the English game of "Brag," poker got its start in New Orleans in 1805, shortly after the Louisiana Purchase. During the steamboat era New Orleans was the site of the most intensive poker games in the world.

POLICE JURY: Same duties as county commissioner in other states.

POORBOY: (See Chapter I, page 12).

PRALINE: A bon bon made of pecans browned in sugar. The name "praline," derived from the name of French marshall and diplomat Cèsar de Plessis Praslin (pronounced "Pra-lin"), later the Duke de Choiseul. It was Marshall Praslin who, according to legend, preferred his almonds cooked in sugar. Since almonds were not readily available to early French inhabitants of Louisiana the meat from the pecan was substituted. Presto! The pecan praline became the most poular confection of our city.

QUADROON: Having one-fourth Negro blood, the child of a mulatto and a Caucasian.

In 1850 Frederick Law Holmsted noted in his writing while in New Orleans that nowhere in the South were more distinct color lines drawn then among the mulattos of Louisiana. So stating, he went on to give this breakdown of the various terms used to designate people with various percentages of Negro blood:

NAME	OFFSPRINGS OF	NEGRO BLOOD
Sacatra	Griffe and Negro	7/8
Griffe	Negro and Mulatto	3/4
Marabou	Mulatto and Griffe	5/8
Mulatto	White and Negro	1/2
Quadroon	White and Mulatto	1/4
Mètif (Octaroon)	White and Quadroon	1/8
Mamelouque	White and Mètif	1/16

SECOND LINE: See "jazz funeral."

SNO/SNOWBALLS: Equivalent to snow cones in other parts of the country.

STORYVILLE: Between the turn of the nineteenth century and World War I there was an area in New Orleans called Storyville. From Basin Street to Claiborne Avenue and from Canal Street to St. Louis, this territory became the official Red Light District set aside by the city for prostitutes to ply their trade.

Sidney Story, an elderman of the city and a righteous man, felt something had to be done to stop the spread of houses of ill repute. After a personally financed tour of major port cities throughout Europe, Story came back to propose to the City Council that it set up a red-light district—not so much to stamp out prostitution but to control it in one area. The City Council liked the idea, passed the ordinance and established the area. When the 3,800 women relegated to that area found out who was responsible for the law they decided to make retribution by naming the area "Storyville" in his honor.

TIGNON: A turban-like, brightly-colored Madras handkerchief, formerly worn by women of color in accordance with a city ordinance.

Many Creole "gentlemen" occupied their spare time with Quadroons and Octaroons as mistresses. The hybrid combinations often resulted in stunning beauty—hair as fine as silk, eyes like serene limpid pools, teeth like cultured pearls. Creole gentlemen had the wherewithal to keep their playthings well-dressed and groomed to perfection. As they went around the city the women were showcases of the latest fashions.

Creole wives were not blind and although they seldom protested to their husbands, they conspired to bring hardship to their competitors. They went to work politically and had an ordinance enacted requiring black females to wear a headdress called the "tignon." Unfortunately for the Creole wives, the strategy backfired. Rather than take away from the beauty of these magnificent women, the tignons served to frame their sculptured faces and bring out their beauty even more. In old photographs and drawings, on dolls and black mammies in front of praline shops in the French Quarter, the tignon is much in evidence.

WHERE Y'AT?: One hundred percent Orleanian, this interrogative arouses much speculation as to how it came about. The most plausible explanation has to do with jazz musicians who would play a gig and then congregate afterwards for jam sessions for their own pleasure. When two musicians met on the way to work they would yell, "Where y'at," meaning, "where are you playing so when I finish my gig I can meet you for a session." As much a part of New Orleans' language today as any slang expression that was born in the city, the question has become entrenched into our vernacular and has evolved into more of a greeting than a query.

The official city seal of 1852 contains 31 stars for 31 states, two Indians, white-bearded Neptune representing the river, and an alligator. (City of New Orleans)

CHAPTER THIRTEEN

Lagniappe

 It is hard to fathom New Orleans without ice to relieve the heat and humidity of its semi-tropical climate and to preserve its food products. Yet this cold commodity was at first a slowly-accepted item; it ultimately became a luxury and a necessity in our community.

According to records the first ice received in New Orleans came in the early 1800s on board a ship from Maine where it had been cut from frozen lakes. Finally there would be relief from the unrelenting heat! Wrong. In fact, ice became a very controversial matter. When the ship arrived in port, New Orleans Mayor Augustine McCarthy, with a police escort, ordered the ice thrown into the river. He had been advised by the city's medical supervisor of its dire consequences: "A cold product taken into the human body would induce tuberculosis." Thank goodness, however, for those aggressive Americans moving into New Orleans; they were always looking for another way to make a fast buck.

The next reference we find regarding ice was in the July 6, 1819, edition of the New Orleans newspaper, *L'Ami-des-Lois*. Richard Salmon was given permission by the City Council to open an ice house after he promised a price unheard of in Southern climates. The insulated building was especially designed to store ice brought in by ship from the Eastern seaboard. Salmon promised in his advertisements to the 27,000 people in the city that business would be conducted on a cash and carry basis at $5.00 per month. Monthly subscribers would get a price break through redeemable coupons, an ice pail in which to carry the treasure home and a cellarett (a case or a sideboard) for storing it. Salmon went to great expense to promote this service but $5.00 per month to subscribers and almost double that for non-subscribers must have been a little too steep. He openly complained in an advertisement of July 14 of the people's lukewarm response to his offer. With ice plentiful he then advertised he would make available another treat: ice cream. But the price was simply not affordable to the people of New Orleans. After July of 1819 newspapers carried no further references to Salmon's ice or ice cream venture either editorially or in the form of advertising.

This failure did not melt the enthusiasm of others as the newspapers were constantly writing of ships arriving with tons of ice. It was risky business for ship captains because of delays at the mouth of the river, not to mention the severe currents encountered coming upstream. It was not uncommon to lose half of the cargo before reaching New Orleans even though the ice was covered with insulating sawdust.

An extreme example of what could happen was revealed in a newspaper article about one ship which left Boston on July 7, 1881, with 1,350 tons of ice. It arrived in New Orleans September 12 with only 800 pounds on board. Needless to say, that ship left a trail of cold water from Boston to the Port of New Orleans.

After 1881 very little is written about ships bringing loads of ice to the city and there was good reason. In 1868 the Louisiana Ice Company located at Delachaise Street and the river went into the business of manufacturing ice commercially. Run by an aggressive, progressive group of seven men and five women, they produced a product superior to the ice from the lakes of the East Coast and sold it for less. Commercially-manufactured ice was clear, much harder, lasted longer and was available year-round.

In just two years the New Orleans Ice Company became a competitor. Located on Howard Avenue and Constance Street, its impressive building was built with three-foot-thick cork walls as insulation and an 80-foot-high ceiling.

With the forces of competition unleased the people could afford the ice now costing $1.75 per hundred pounds. Demand caused by the 1878 Yellow Fever epidemic drove prices up to $300 per hundred weight but as this calamity passed an increasing number of firms entered the business and by the turn of the century prices were pretty stable at 25¢ for a 100 pounds, 15¢ for 50 pounds, and 10¢ for 25 pounds. Meat markets, which could not afford large quantities of ice, would buy just enough to keep the meat cool during the day. In the evenings at closing time, under special contract, they would bring their supply to the ice house for overnight storage.

Soon, home delivery was being offered. If no one was home at the time of delivery drivers left a quantity of ice determined by the size of an empty milk bottle left on the front steps. If someone was at home delivery was made directly into the house and into the ice box. Competitive drivers also emptied the pans catching the water as it melted under the refrigerator. A favorite summer pastime of children was to follow the wagons and sneak a small chip of cracked ice when the driver left the wagon to make a delivery.

Just as the steam locomotive replaced the steamboat, and gasoline-driven buses put an end to the streetcars as masters of city transportation, we find the introduction of the mechanical refrigerator in the 1930s as the beginning of the end to all but the best-managed commercial ice houses in New Orleans. Lessened demand for ice resulted in a price war that reduced the price from $10.00 to $1.00 a ton. Separating the wheat from the chaff, only a few commercial houses survive today.

Pelican Ice Company, formally New Orleans Ice Company, is the second-oldest ice company in the United States. Founded in 1870, it has continued in business for over a century. The same building, with its three-foot-thick walls insulated with cork and 80-foot-high ceilings, is still producing that much-needed product in our city. Understandably, the mule stable located near the main building was torn down and put to more contemporary use. Mules were not only used for making home deliveries but also as a source of power. They drove the pulleys to stack the ice up to the 80-foot ceiling, thereby ensuring a large enough reserve to allow delivery orders as large as 100 tons on demand.

The oldest operating ice house in North America has survived because of its adaptability to the times. Today, Pelican Ice is
open 24 hours a day, 365 days a year.

Large orders are still filled but not quite as frequently. Re-
cently NASA ordered 60 tons of ice to simulate a blizzard for test-
ing purposes. In 1982 a Canadian ski resort sent a team of snow ski
instructors to give lessons to New Orleanians on Audubon Park's
Monkey Hill. Pelican Ice covered the ski slope with approximately
20 tons of man-made snow.

When you tell Pelican Ice to "Cool it," they simply ask how
many tons, where you want it delivered and when.

SNO (SNOW) BALLS

Although you will not find the definition of New Orleans sno
(snow) balls in the dictionary they are as much a part of New

A 1930 drawing of a portable snowball stand by George A. Pearce.

Orleans as red beans and rice, poor-boys, muffuletta sandwiches, the terms "Where ya at?" and banquette. In fact, New Orleans is the undisputed world capital for snoballs. And we don't mean snow cones, those miserable cone-shaped chunks of ice doused with thin spearmint, strawberry or grape syrup and sold at fairs and circuses throughout the country. New Orleans snoballs, with shaved ice and rich-flavored syrups, are enjoyed by Orleanians with the same intensity as a good bowl of gumbo. While snoballs have no nutritional value and are sprinkled with sugar-coated calories by the thousands, they are celebrated in our city because they are colorful, they taste good and on humid summer days they feel fantastic. Yes, they're New Orleans!

Sometimes historians run across popular local traditions that cannot be attributed to a specific person or persons or assigned a special date of inception. It's been difficult to pin down specifics about snoballs.

In 1897 Woodward Wright and Company issued a catalogue displaying ice picks, ice chisels, ice axes and tongs plus a Gem Ice Shaver with an adjustable blade to shave ice as thinly as desired. Old timers in their 80's seem to think that the cooling tradition was popularized around the 1920s.

To my way of thinking, the king and queen of New Orleans snoballs are Ernest and Mary Hansen of Hansen's Snobliz Shop on the corner of Tchoupitoulas and Bordeaux Streets. In 1934 Ernest invented and patented the Snobliz machine which has been in use ever since. From secret formulas Mary produces the finest syrups. Together, the machine, the ice and Mary's creations produce a piece of New Orleans that has never been duplicated.

While Ernest kept his invention for himself, George Ortalano, who owned a grocery store at Magazine and Delachaise Streets, developed the Sno Wizzard, sold it commercially and revolutionized the art of making this refresher. While the grocery store is gone, George, his wife, Josie and son Anthony operate the Sno Wizzard Manufacturing Company on the same site.

Unfortunately, snoballs have not caught on in other states but they remain an institution in our city known for its uniqueness. It is interesting to note that the three most popular colors/flavors—purple/grape, green/spearmint, and gold/lemon—are the three colors of Mardi Gras. Coincidence? Perhaps . . .

DOLL HOUSE

In 1915 Gabe Hausmann, Sr. (of Hausmann's Jewelry) built his family home at the corner of St. Charles Avenue and Broadway. At the same time he was building the family home he had his contractor erect a miniature doll house of the same materials and design for his daughter, Theone.

Large enough to comfortably accommodate four children, Theone and her little friends could play in the house day or night; it was wired and had electrical fixtures along with doll furniture, colorful rugs, curtains in the windows and awnings over the windows and the door. A back porch added later provided even more enjoyment for Theone and company.

For the house, a symbol of love from father to daughter, Hausmann obtained an official street number to facilitate delivery of mail from himself to his daughter at her own address.

After 69 years the family home still stands alongside Theone's doll house. The maintenance man assigned for many years to the premises also did necessary repairs to the minature replica which was later used by Theone's sister and still later by Theone's niece.

As an expression of his love, Gabe Hausmann built a miniature replica of his home as a doll house for his daughter Theone. (Photo by Don Knecht)

ALLIGATORS IN THE CITY LIMITS!!!
BY THE THOUSANDS!!!

In 1726 John Pierre Lassus, surveyor and artist, drew one of

In 1726, Jean Pierre Lassus completed the earliest-known New Orleans painting. At bottom center a man can be seen shoving a pole down the mouth of a large alligator. (The Historic New Orleans Collection)

the first pictures of New Orleans. In the center foreground of the picture is a man shoving a pole down an alligator's mouth. The alligator in the picture is much larger than the man. Today, as in the early 1700s, alligators still can be found in large numbers within the city limits.

In the 1800s the New Orleans city guide gave considerable detail on hunting alligators. During the Civil War, when leather was not available, alligator hides were used to replace leather with outstanding results. Since then alligator skins have been used for shoes, wallets, belts, purses and other wearing apparel. When taken from the tail, alligator flesh is considered by some to be as good as meat from any other creature.

In 1982, during a one-month period, 96 alligators were killed in only 50 square miles of marshland in New Orleans East during the legal alligator hunting season. And New Orleans has roughly 182 square miles of marshes and waterways. Some of the gators still lurking within the city limits are quite large. In September 1982, on Chef Menteur Highway across from Halter Marine Co., a 12'7" long, 500-pound alligator was killed.

Nearer the heart of town in City Park, with its eight miles of lagoons, there have been alligator sightings for as many years as the Park has been in existence. Not too long ago it was feared that thieves were stealing ducks from the lagoons. Surveillance determined they were being taken (not stolen) by alligators.

As to how many alligators presently live within the city limits, no one can say. But consider these facts:

1. Approximately 182 square miles of canals or marshes in the city limits provide excellent habitats for alligators;
2. Supposedly, there are an estimated five alligators per square mile, which is a very conservative estimate considering they lay from 35 to 75 eggs per year;
3. Alligators have been an endangered and protected species since 1963;
4. Once reaching three feet in length the gator's only enemy is man, from whom it is legally protected.

If for some reason alligators become extinct, they will still be remembered as a part of New Orleans: the official seal of the city, authorized on June 18, 1852, features a large alligator at bottom center. And the largest figure on the official 1984 World's Fair poster, which is expected to sell in the hundreds of thousands, is of an alligator.

Since there is no known way to tell an alligator's age it is just possible that some of them have been around since New Orleans was founded.

Yes, New Orleans is still inhabited by alligators, as evidenced by this 12-foot, 500-pounder killed by Joe Madere on September 13, 1982 within the city limits. (Photo compliments of Joe Madere)

Appropriately named "Lagniappe," this brief chapter—although not essential to the structure of this book—was nonetheless included to illustrate the nature of the term and the nature of the New Orleans personality.

When a wide-eyed New Orleans child asks the candy store owner for a 25-cent piece of praline, and the proprietor adds a couple of jelly beans and a piece of bubble gum as "Lagniappe," the bonus is not a contingency. But it adds a nice touch to the transaction . . . and encourages the customer to come back for more.

Tout à vous! (At your service!)